Make the Choices Now to Give Yourself the Future You Want!

"What, I ask you, could be more rightly thrilling than seeing yourself change right in front of your own eyes? Not a superficial, temporary change, but a permanent, fundamental change in the kind of person you are! If your heart has yearned for a practical, powerful guide which cuts right through the nonsense and which, in plain language, goes straight to the heart of what to do to start being a new and higher you, this book has everything you need to get you started—today!"

— Dr. Stephen Hamby, Ph.D.

"Some of the most powerful reading I have experienced. The ideas and exercises are extremely self-changing. I am amazed at the glimpses of mental clarity I have experienced."

— Marc Whitman, AIA

"In this book you'll be given the secret keys that put you in command of your life journey and all of its experiences. You will learn how to design your own destiny. There are such secrets. They are real. They can be yours!"

— Ken Roberts
author of *A Rich Man's Secret*

About the Author

Guy Finley is the author of over eight books and books-on-tape, several of which have become international bestsellers. His writings are found in public libraries throughout the United States and his work is widely endorsed by doctors, celebrities, and leading professionals. He has enjoyed numerous successful careers, including composing award-winning music for many popular recording artists, motion pictures, and television programs.

In 1979, after travels to India and parts of the Far East in search of truth and higher wisdom, Guy voluntarily retired from his flourishing career in order to simplify his life and continue with his inner studies. He now lives in southern Oregon, where he gives ongoing talks on self-development.

To Write to the Author

Guy Finley lives and teaches in southern Oregon, where he speaks twice weekly about higher self-development. If you would like to write him about this book or wish more information about his other works, please send a self-addressed stamped envelope to: Guy Finley

P.O. Box 10-D

Merlin, OR 97532

Visit Guy Finley's Life of Learning Foundation web site at:

www.guyfinley.com

Take part in his discovery-filled monthly chat room discussions, enjoy excerpts from his books, and get the latest news on continuing developments and special in-person appearances.

GUY FINLEY

DESIGN YOUR DESTINY

Shape Your Future in 12 Easy Steps

1999
Llewellyn Publications
St. Paul, Minnesota 55164-0383, U.S.A.

Second Edition
First printing, 1999
(Previously titled *Designing Your Own Destiny*)

First edition, two printings, 1995

Design Your Destiny was originally published as *The Key of Kings* under a special licensing agreement with 4 Star Books, a division of the Ken Roberts Company. The first edition of *The Key of Kings* was published in November 1993.

Cover art and design: Lisa Novak
Book design and editing: Kimberly Nightingale

Library of Congress Cataloging-in-Publication Data
Design your destiny : shape your future in 12 easy steps / Guy Finley—2nd ed.
p.   cm.
Rev. ed. of: Designing your own destiny. 1995.
Includes bibliographical references.
ISBN 1-56718-282-8
1. Success—Psychological aspects.   2. Self-efficacy.   3. Self-actualization
(Psychology)   I. Finley, Guy, 1949-   Designing your own destiny.
II. Title.
BF637.S8F55   1999
158'.1--DC21   99-31573
                                                                      CIP

Llewellyn Publications
A Division of Llewellyn Worldwide, Ltd.
P.O. Box 64383, Dept. K282-8
St. Paul, MN 55164-0383
www.llewellyn.com

Printed in the United States of America

Other Books by Guy Finley

The Secret of Letting Go
The Secret Way of Wonder
Freedom from the Ties that Bind
The Intimate Enemy
The Lost Secrets of Prayer

Books-On-Tape

The Secret of Letting Go

Cassette Tape Sets

The Road to Good Fortune
The Lost Secrets of Prayer
Only the Fearless Are Free
7 Characteristics of Higher Consciousness
Secrets of Cleansing Your Heart, Mind & Soul

Videotape Sets

Forgotten Practices for Self-Awakening
Secrets of Cleansing Your Heart, Mind & Soul

Booklets

30 Keys to Change Your Destiny
5 Steps to Complete Freedom from Stress

Dedication

To those for whom the Good is all things.

A Special Note to the Reader

To receive your free encouraging poster of helpful inner-life insights as well as information on Guy Finley's books, tapes, and ongoing classes, write to:

The Life of Learning Foundation
P.O. Box 10-D
Merlin, OR 97532

To receive your free copy of *30 Keys to Change Your Destiny*, a powerful pocketbook version of the inner-life exercises in *Designing Your Destiny*, plus nineteen more fascinating self-discoveries, send a self-addressed stamped envelope along with $1 (Outside U.S.A., $3 U.S. funds) to the address listed above.

Help spread the Light! If you know of someone who is interested in these higher ideas, please send his or her name and address to The Life of Learning Foundation at the above address. The latest complete list of Guy Finley's books, booklets, and tapes will be sent to them. Thank you!

CONTENTS

PART THREE:
SUCCESS THROUGH
HIGHER SELF-STUDIES

Foreword
by Ken Roberts

Great men are they who see that
the spiritual is stronger than
material force, that thoughts rule
the world.

—Ralph Waldo Emerson

WHY DID YOU PICK UP THIS BOOK?

Could it be that somewhere in your heart you long to understand Emerson's statement? That within you is that uncommon wish to dwell in the undisturbed depths of your own true nature, above the tempests of a world filled with heartache and confusion?

If your answer is "yes," and I trust that it is, maybe you'd like to know what's next. Maybe you've been wondering what you can do to awaken that great power that is the foundation of inner health, wealth, and peace.

You can start by preparing yourself for a series of powerful and life-changing self-discoveries! For this book you're holding is actually a special kind of bridge that will deliver you to the real answers—and strengths you've been seeking. Here at last is a book that teaches, directly, what you can do to find what is genuinely life-changing. In a way, you now stand at that same intersection where Robert Frost once found himself, and later wrote of, in his timeless verse about personal choice:

> *Two roads diverged in a wood, and I*
> *I took the one less traveled by,*
> *And that has made all the difference.*
>
> *—The Road Not Taken*

These pages written by Guy Finley comprise a very unique guide for the sincere seeker of the higher life. It can lead you through that elusive transition from working with helpful ideas to the actual discovery—the experience—of a higher world within you.

You'll gain conscious access to that interior part of your own psyche where your actual life experience is being created from one moment to the next. Yes, this book is for those who desire to cross that secret bridge; the one that leads directly to a powerful new awareness that fears no circumstance because it is in total command of its own destiny. Doesn't this sound just like the kind of life you've always hoped for but never dared dreamed was possible?

I assure you, such an uncompromising life can be yours. All you need to succeed is some new, true knowledge—anchored with your sincere wish to be all that your heart of hearts is urging you to be.

At this point maybe you're asking, What kind of new knowledge has the power to deliver me to such a fearless life?

For a brief look into the bright new self-understanding that awaits you, allow me to refer you to one of Guy's earlier best-selling works, *The Secret of Letting Go* (Llewellyn, 1994). In this classic self-development book, Guy relates the little-known story of how Genghis Khan, the historically infamous Mongol warlord, defeated many of his enemies from within their own ranks by using psychological warfare. In fact, as amazing at it may seem, some of Khan's victories were achieved without a battle! Let's see how he accomplished this, then we'll learn how our new knowledge can help to positively transform our present situation.

Khan would send specially trained agents in advance of his own approaching army. These people would dress and pose as common peasants in order to infiltrate the enemy's camp. Once accepted as locals who were loyal and apparently belonged there, Khan's secret agents would talk to the people encamped there, spreading alarming stories about the vast size, fierceness, and invincibility of Khan's forces. Since these tales of terror appeared to be coming from their own people—who had no reason to lie—the soldiers and other camp followers accepted the stories as the truth, which meant there was no other choice in the face of such insurmountable odds.

The only wise thing to do was to surrender to Khan and hope for mercy.

What do you think? Does something seem strangely familiar about this bit of history? It should; there's an ongoing story in our own psyche similar to this one. Yes, we're being deceived and misdirected daily by our present way of thinking. But the light of a new and higher understanding can free us from this deception and all its sad defeats. And this means . . . we can have a new destiny if we so choose.

If you're anything like me, and feel as I did when first coming to discover that all my defeats in life were an "inside job," maybe your wish to know more about yourself just got a little stronger. Good! That's all it takes for now. Ignore those parts of yourself telling you that trying to change your destiny with only a wish for a higher life is like trying to climb Mt. Everest with a stepladder. Instead of submitting to these inner voices of defeat, use your energies to consider the following.

Think for just a moment about what's involved in simply tying a shoelace. Now consider the task of trying to write a comprehensive set of instructions for this relatively easy physical task. Seems overwhelming—almost an impossibility—doesn't it? And yet, five-year-olds rather quickly learn to tie their own shoelaces in spite of the odds. Why? Because they don't think about and dwell upon the intricacies of the job they're undertaking. They just naturally respond to their own paramount wish to be able to tie their own shoelaces. That one wish is all they need to realize their dream and desire. And so it is that your wish for a higher life attracts to you all that you need to succeed, too. In fact, you may not realize this yet, but it's that very wish that has placed this special book into your hands.

So, don't stop now! Work with Guy Finley's principles, apply the practices, study the insights, and embrace the exercises. Look upon them as though they can help you to start your whole life over again on a higher and happier level. For they can. Do this special inner work—as outlined—and then you'll know:

Designing your destiny is the greatest pleasure on earth. For once you know the secret of how to choose in favor of what is true, you also know, forever, how to choose in favor of you.

Ken Roberts is founder and CEO of a
multinational financial education company.

PART ONE

Getting Started

Chapter One

Why You Should Feel Encouraged

LEARNING HOW TO DESIGN YOUR DESTINY is not like learning to repair a clock or master a new language. So it's important to realize—right here at the outset—that if it takes time to develop and perfect even such common skills as these, how much more so is asked of those of us who would learn how to shape our own future!

That's why you must be patient with yourself. And I assure you with the study material you're about to read, your patience will be rewarded. In the pages that follow, you'll encounter some ideas and insights that you've probably never considered before. In fact, I'm sure you haven't. The keys in this book are to inner doors that few have suspected existed—let alone thought to open and enter. But you can succeed. In fact, you may not know it yet, but you've already taken your first steps toward something higher.

How?

Just by having this material in your hands, your destiny is already new and different. I'll explain.

That part of yourself that led you to acquire this book already belongs to an existing higher line of destiny within you. That's correct. The wish itself—to be a higher person—comes to you from a higher place and is received in its inner equivalent within you. This means there's already an existing connection between the you that you want to be and the you that you presently are; between the new destiny you would have, and the fortunes you've known. All you have to do is stay on the royal road that has brought you up to this very point, for it leads directly to that higher destiny you seek. And now you're about to begin another leg of your appointed journey.

There's so much ahead of you that's new and exciting. But you must remember that the best views are always the higher ones, whose new heights take personal effort to achieve. To ensure you'll make steady progress along this higher way, allow me to instruct and encourage you in two special ways.

First, as you proceed with these new life lessons about winning the higher life, you may come to certain moments where you have a disquieting feeling that you don't understand what you're doing or, for that matter, even why you're doing it! But each time you get ready to throw your hands up in the air or toss in the towel, do your best to remember the following. For as strange as this may seem to you as you stand there, feeling oh-so uncertain, here's the true perspective to be embraced: These are the good times, not the bad ones! In fact, all along you've been working toward just these moments.

How can this be possible? Your confusion indicates that you have reached a real inner threshold; you stand before the possibility of entering into something genuinely new to you. And this unthinkable place is the same as the doorway to a new destiny. So take heart!

Second, if you'll simply persist with your journey, you'll pass right through these times of trial. I guarantee it. Nothing can stop your sincere inquiry, including those thoughts and feelings telling you that you can't go any further because you don't understand how to take the next step. Take that step anyway. Then you'll understand.

The light from one small moment of honest self-inquiry is more powerful than the accumulated darkness of a million years of doubt. So dare to proceed . . . and succeed!

Special Summary

All uncertainty is life's special invitation to enter the mystery of the ever-new—and once within this timeless world to discover yourself there as its keeper.

Chapter Two

A Special Invitation to Be One of the Few

FOR AS LONG AS MEN AND WOMEN HAVE walked this great earth, they've been unlocking the mysteries of the world around them. It is our nature to delve, discover, and push the limits of the known. One by one, from fire to fusion, we have patiently but persistently coerced Mother Nature's great secrets out into the open and into our service.

But for all our insights and conquests over the forces of life around us, we are still living very much in the dark when it comes to understanding the nature of those forces that dwell within us.

What about this uncharted world within? What do we really know of its oceans of surging emotions? Of its countless invisible forms of thought? And yet, when put to question, few are troubled to admit it's these same unseen forces at work in this inner world that actually determines the way in which our outer one turns, which makes the following all the harder to understand: Why does this essential world, which exists in the very heart of us, go unsought and so superficially examined?

With so much to gain, with so many powers to be uncovered like layers of treasure in a sunken chest, why are there so few who will dare to probe—and so possess—all the breathtaking and self-empowering secrets of their own innermost self?

This book is your invitation to be one of the few. In your hands are all the instructions you need to make the journey to this invisible world within and, upon your safe arrival, to take possession and command of your own thoughts and feelings. What an adventure awaits you once you gain the powers needed to design your destiny.

In our travels and studies together, we're going to find out why so much of our daily direction seems to come out of default. Why does it seem that when we really want to do—or to be—something truly new and different, we almost always wind up doing just the opposite; where instead of meeting the greater challenge, we find ourselves taking the path of least resistance, and then either blaming someone or something for our condition; or else sadly resenting ourselves for our own weakness. Instead of meeting the greater challenge, we find ourselves taking the path of least resistance. We blame either someone or something for our condition or sadly resent ourselves for our own weakness.

If you've had enough of being too much for yourself, *Design Your Destiny* holds all the tools you need to discover, and then call upon, a new source of strength that will make you the ruler of your own life. In this book, you'll be given the secret keys that put you in command of your life journey, as well as all its experiences. You will learn how to determine your own destiny. There are such secrets. They are real. And they can be yours.

In the twelve powerful inner-life steps that are the heart and body of this book, you'll discover how to become conscious of, and completely master, both the strong and subtle forces that determine your life choices. And since it is these life choices, your daily decisions, that ultimately decide your direction in life, becoming conscious of the invisible inner influences that determine these decisions will be the same as taking into your hands the reins of your own destiny.

Repeat: You can learn how to be that rarest of individuals who is always going exactly where he or she wants to be going; one whose entire life experience—each and every step along the chosen way—never fails to be self-enriching. This is the life that's intended to be your destiny! Let's gather the facts that will deliver its realization.

Special Summary

To go beyond yourself, you must first be yourself. To be yourself takes no special understanding, only a willingness to see yourself as you really are.

Chapter Three

Design Your Destiny

IT IS A LAW NOT OF MAN'S OR WOMAN'S but of life: Before you can have a different life; before you can be happier, wiser, more at peace, and in quiet command of yourself, you must first be different. Being is everything.

What is Being?

A moment's consideration helps determine that everything around us has some form of Being. Why is this true?

Because all physical forms—whether animated or not—are expressions of that one great life whose vast intelligent and creative energies are the foundation of all we perceive. So we can reason that even a common rock has being of a sort. Similarly, all manner of beings—from rocks to roses, to you and I (all unique expressions of this one great energy)—possess a nature.

What Gives Something Its Nature?

The nature of a rock is determined entirely by the natural forces acting upon it. This means its Being is without any choice; which further means that both the rock's nature—and its destiny—are, in fact, predetermined. One day it will be dust. The gradual disintegration is part of the nature of all things physical.

And neither does the rose, dressed so delicately in its fragrant velveteen petals, have a choice as to its nature. An individual rose can't choose not to have thorns or attract bees. Like the rock next to which it grows, the nature of any rose is a fixed expression of its being.

But human nature—your nature—is not fixed. It can be transformed.

This amazing quality, the inherent potential mutability of our nature, is what sets us above all God's countless other creations. And this fact about our unique nature also empowers us in a very special way. As a feature of our Being, each of us is created with the power to choose the course of our own destiny. Let's see how this is possible.

Your Being is in a constant process of unfolding. That it will unfold is not your choice. Being is a gift that came with birth. It is. And while Being is both the creator and cosmic animator of your individual story, how your life unfolds—the direction it takes—is something you can influence. It's called making choices. And being empowered to have a real voice in your life choices is what this book is all about. See if the following makes perfect sense.

Before you can change the course of and learn to design your destiny, you must first gain access to that secret place within yourself where your own future is being created moment by moment by moment. Yes, there is such a location. It's real. And yes, you can learn to dwell there and direct your destiny.

This truly timeless place, where all your life choices are made for you, is what we understand, in concept, as the present moment. But this state of true now is not just an idea. It's a place of extraordinary and measureless power, for the true present moment is actually a cosmic seed of a sort, from out of which springs all that comes later. And this point brings us to one of our key lessons.

Coupled with the new knowledge you've already gained from this study, your close consideration of the following insight will bring you one step closer to taking command of your own destiny. The present moment is where our being, which is a timeless unconditioned energy, meets and animates our nature. Now our nature, on the other hand, lives only in time; meaning it's fabricated from all our past experiences. Said slightly differently, our nature is a psychological body of memories and knowledge structured by our social, economic, and religious conditioning.

The present moment, where our being and our nature meet, is the instant of our destiny. And up until now, we've had little real choice in how our fates unfold because it's always been our nature— our accumulated past with all of its fears, compulsions, and doubts—that has been running the show. Just a few more facts will help us to further understand some of the inherent problems built into this unconscious inner condition.

Our present nature is a thought nature. It must think to know itself. And because the only way it can know itself is through thought, this mental nature is unable to see that many of its own thoughts are not what it thinks them to be. For instance, we've all known a certain thought that told us we were strong or that our life was "really together." But later we found ourselves badly shocked at the depth of our own self-deception.

Reality came along, as it always does, and made us see that our image of ourselves was just that; only a thought with no real strength at all!

Repetitive experiences such as these should make it clear enough. Our present nature can't know when it's reached a bad decision because in that moment—as it's busy deciding our destiny using its own confused or misguided understanding—our nature is, itself, that bad choice. Not only can't it see the forest for the trees, sometimes this nature doesn't even know it's lost in the woods!

Things would be bleak indeed if there were no other choice but to live out the remainder of our lives under the conditions imposed by this limited consciousness. Our day-to-day life-situation would not be too dissimilar from that of being a passenger in a coach drawn by six powerful horses with no driver to steer it! Yes, we would, no doubt, be able to get from one place to the next. But for the whole ride we would be nervous and uncertain not only about where we were headed, but also if we would arrive there at all! Sound familiar? I know it does! And our agreement serves to take us on to the next step in our journey. Perhaps the most pivotal one.

The time has come to introduce a third character to the horse and carriage metaphor. You're about to be introduced to a force in your own consciousness that, when brought to bear in each and every moment of meeting between your nature and your being, produces both the missing driver and the reins you need to begin designing your destiny.

You can think of this third force that you can command as a kind of special window into the present moment. It's called awareness. And it is the most unique feature of your nature for the following reason: Your awareness of the present moment is the present moment.

You can, and should, pause here for a moment to breathe some life into this very important idea. To take it out of the realm of thought and into your direct experience, just choose to become fully aware of yourself.

If you've never tried this before, here are some helpful guidelines.

Come wide awake to your total environment this moment. Just know, without thinking, what are all the sounds, sights, feelings, thoughts, impressions, textures, and temperatures around and within you right now. Again, this knowing yourself and your surroundings is not arrived at by going into thought. And if you practice this higher kind of self-presence, you'll see that this special awareness of yourself is the same as the present moment in which you just became aware. They are one and the same. Which means this self-awareness, as it includes the present moment, is also a feature of your Being. This is the inner realization we've been working toward all along.

Your awareness of the present moment, which is a secret part of your true being, doesn't have to think about which direction is best for you. It knows because it sees. Where your usual nature is often blinded by its own unseen self-interests, your Being, represented in the moment by your awareness of it, effortlessly sees into—and through—this unconsciously compromised thinking even as it's occurring.

The presence of this higher intelligence keeps you from defeating yourself. And this is the same as making you newly victorious! For each time you have the awareness not to choose from that bank of old patterns produced by your limited thought nature, new and higher alternatives appear before your inner eyes. These moments, and their messages, rise to greet you from your true Being. And with these directions as your guide, designing your destiny is as effortless as you are now confident— for how can you not succeed when reality itself points your way!

Special Comment

For extra important benefits, please read the above section over at least once again, or until you know you're beginning to understand the new concepts it presents. It goes without saying that some of the special insights offered in this and following sections of the book can be challenging; but it needs to be said that these discoveries are not beyond your reach if you'll risk the temporary discomfort of stretching for something that seems to exceed your present grasp. But all is closer than you think! Here's why this is true.

The ideas in this book are based in reality, which is the same as saying they're accessible to anyone who wills to see them. Stated slightly differently, your success with these ideas all depends upon the strength of your wish to see beyond what your present understanding says it's possible for you to see. But when you can also see that your present level of understanding can't know there is something real beyond it, then you know what must be done to win that new and higher understanding.

So dare to reach beyond yourself and hold that wish out there until the new ground you would stand upon rises up beneath you. It will, if you will.

Special Summary

The great power in true self-awareness is that nothing can come into it without its complete character being revealed upon its entrance.

Chapter Four

Taking the High Road that Leads to Self-Rule

FOLLOWING THIS LAST, BRIEF SECTION, you'll be introduced to twelve steps especially created to help you master the inner skills needed to design your destiny. Each one has unique properties and presents stimulating interior challenges that will help you awaken new levels of higher self-awareness. With alert practice, you'll soon possess the power to change the direction of your life—by changing your nature—as it expresses itself in the present moment.

For best results, read the twelve steps all the way through, just as you would read any book from start to finish. Then return to the individual lessons by making each one the focus of your undivided study for at least a full day.

For superior results, I suggest you work with each step for one complete week. Take longer if you like. But regardless of your elected length of practice time, make every effort with each step to work with its particular inner lessons at every available opportunity . . . of which you're sure to find dozens in any twelve-hour period.

Start with any one of the steps. Maybe there is one that better suits your personal situation at the moment than another. That's fine. Whichever step you choose to begin your inner work, it's important that you work all the way through each of the twelve.

Here is one last suggested instruction that will help your inner work progress noticeably faster:

As you finish working with one step and prepare to move on to the next, continue with the practice of the one you've just completed. Even though the new step on your list will demand most of your attention, you can remain aware of—and continue to work on—these combined studies. You'll discover that the collective effect of these steps supports and amplifies one another in ways that help hasten higher self-discovery.

One last note: Succeed just once—with any of these unique inner life steps—and your life will never be the same again. All will be new for you; both for the fact of your victory over your own time nature, and for your new knowing that now tells you . . . you can design your destiny!

Special Summary

There is no such thing as a wasted step when your final destination is self-transformation.

PART TWO

How To Design Your Destiny

Chapter Five

Step 1:
Get One Thing Done

Special Insight

NEVER MIND HOW MUCH THERE MAY
be to do; or how hard some task
appears to be.

Get one thing done and then take
that step again. Consciously brush aside
any other concerns. Do what's in your
power. Refuse to deal with what's not.

The Road Before You

Have you ever had this experience? You're faced with so many things that have to be done in a timely manner that it overwhelms you . . . so all you do is nothing! Well, that is, almost nothing. You do manage to:

- Worry yourself sick about how you'll get everything done.

- Eat or snack until you feel drowsy.

- Take several naps hoping to awaken inspired.

- Reorganize your papers and desk drawers as part of your plan of attack.

- Worry about all the time you've wasted making plans and reorganizing your desk.

If you're tired of finding yourself exhausted—even before you're able to start working on some line of tasks assembled before you—this exercise is custom-made for you.

The following insights and prescribed actions will lend just the help you need to succeed in handling a hundred pressing jobs; all while enjoying that inner calm and confidence that comes with knowing that you're not only doing all that can be done, but you're also doing it in the best manner!

You might be familiar with that time-tested golden adage "All is not as it appears to be." One of the hard ways we've all learned that this old say-ing is true is when it comes to encountering certain smiling faces. There's no doubt about it. Appear-ances can and often do deceive.

But we've yet to discover that this same wise advice also holds true to the appearance of our own thoughts. Thoughts deceive us all the time. It's true. In fact, people deceive us because we let our own ideas about that person mislead us. We see a smiling person and assume that person is friendly. But it's not just in the area of relationships that our own thoughts deceive and betray us. Which brings us to the key insight underlying this exercise.

At any given moment, regardless of appearance or emotional certainty to the contrary, it is not the demand of those already-overdue, one-hundred-and-one tasks that have you feeling so overwhelmed and under prepared. What you're really experienc-ing is the overwhelming presence of one thought. One thought that calls itself "one-hundred-and-one things to do." Impossible, you say? Read on.

The power that this one thought has to deceive—and to ultimately freeze you in your tracks—is born partly out of its invisible alliance with anxiety-laden emotions. Here's how these two terrible tricksters team up to keep you off track and forever running for the train. Thoughts have the power to present themselves to your mind in picture form. These thoughts are known to us and experienced as imagination. In this instance, as it concerns our study, one thought assumes the image, or mental picture, of one-hundred-and-one tasks yet to be completed. To illustrate to you how this kind of mental picture is possible, imagine a photograph of a terribly cluttered desk. This mental picture is, in fact, one image with a thousand loose ends!

What happens next is that this single mental picture, consisting of multiple superimposed images, becomes animated with anxious and pressure-filled feelings. Now in your mind's eye, that picture of your impossible situation not only looks real . . . it feels that way too! But this show has just begun.

In the wink of an eye, a second thought pops up. And unbeknownst to you, it's in league with the initial imaginary scene projected by the first thought. Its task is to confirm your worst suspicions; which it does when it announces in a small but defeated voice that sounds a lot like your own "It's hopeless. There's just too much to do. How can I get out of this?"

Choosing Your New Direction

The next time you "hear" this inner voice of imminent doom, listen instead to this higher instruction: Never again look for a way out of any anxious condition. Look instead for a way to see through it.

Now learn the higher techniques that will show you how to be a self-starting individual instead of a self-stalling one.

Each time you're faced with a logjam of tasks that seem far beyond your mortal abilities to resolve in the allotted time, here's what to do. First, whittle these logs down to manageable size by writing each one out on a pad of paper. This act will also help you untangle some of your own tangled feelings about the jam you're in. For now, forget their order of importance; that will become clear later. Just get each task down on paper. Besides, your priorities can only be as clear as your thinking, so making this list helps to clarify both. Another benefit of your list is that it will keep confusion out of the picture, and confusion is to anxiety what wind is to a dust devil.

Once you have your list of tasks written down on paper, place a star next to number one on your list. Then do it! What does this mean? Exactly what it says!

Take number one on your list and just get that one thing done. Consciously refuse to entertain any other thoughts that push themselves into your mind with images of impossibility. It is possible to do one thing at a time. And it is possible to successfully complete one thing at a time, and to do that one thing to the very best of your ability.

Then . . . move to the next task at hand: number two. Follow the same winning procedure as you did with number one. Then do number three and so on until all is done.

Your Higher Destiny

The main lesson here is that success only becomes impossible when you try to deal with what isn't in your power. Renegade parts of you want you to waste your powers dealing with them. Your misguided attention to their punishing presence gives them a life they wouldn't have without tricking you into giving them one. This means you don't need power to deal with what's been defeating you, only the higher understanding it takes to consciously dismiss it from your inner life. You have that power now. Start using it.

Work with this step. Use its instructions. Get one thing done, one at a time, all the way down your list . . . whatever it may be. Proceed in spite of any thoughts or feelings that would have you believe you can't. Just behind your certainty that your "list" is too much for you lies a new and conscious capability to proceed one step at a time, to accomplish one task at a time, to your satisfaction.

Special Summary

The most beautiful tapestry in the world begins and ends with but one of a hundred-thousand threads.

Doubt is the vestibule which all must pass before they can enter the temple of Wisdom. When we are in doubt and puzzle out the truth by our own exertions, we have gained something that will stay by us and serve us again. But, if to avoid the trouble of the search we avail ourselves of the superior information of a friend, such knowledge will not remain with us; we have not bought, but borrowed it.

—Caleb Colton

Chapter Six

Step 2:
Take the Conscious Risk

Special Insight

NOTHING YOU'RE AFRAID OF LOSING
can ever be the source of your fearlessness.

The Road Before You

Has there ever been a time in your
life—a period of real self-enriching
growth—that wasn't connected to a
risk you either willingly undertook
or—to a time of inner trial where there

was no other choice for you but to take a risk? Of course, there's only one answer to this question, and its one recognized as being true wherever you may ask it in the world: The prize of greater wisdom and inner strength always goes to those who take, in one way or another, the risk.

But one note before we go any further. I am not recommending risking your resources on ridiculous "get-rich-quick" financial schemes. Nor am I recommending risking your life by trying to cheat death with some harebrained stunt. These kinds of activities aren't really risks at all, other than on a very superficial level. Yes, risks like these may give you a temporary charge, but so does sticking your finger in an electrical socket! Real self-change goes far beyond boosting self-esteem. It's a permanent inner transformation that frees you from feeling low in the first place.

This step is specialized instruction, a higher education, in how it's possible for you to find—and then willingly enter into—conscious risks. With what you're about to learn, you won't have to wait for an accidental or painful event to come along and prompt you into realizing a self-liberating self-change.

You'll be empowered with a secret knowledge that will actually allow you to choose these moments of self-transformation. You will have a hand in creating your own destiny and ultimate spiritual success.

Let's take a moment to briefly review what is a conscious risk and why these kinds of risks can be such a powerful catalyst for inner change. Then we'll learn how to locate these special risks at will, including the winning actions to take when these moments of conscious risk present themselves. But first, a definition: A conscious risk involves making a choice to do what's true, in spite of what that choice may cost you.

One fairly common example of this uncommon kind of inner valor is refusing to go along with the destructive behavior of someone you love—even though that choice may mean he or she walks out of your life. But even here the victory is still yours. For even in the worst-case scenarios, you always discover that what you lose is never the thing you feared losing.

Yes, that self-destructive man or woman may be gone for good, which hurts at first. But it's not too long before you know something else is missing too. What you really lost was a part of yourself that had been a secret slave to a false image of what it means to be loving—or to the fear of finding yourself alone. And as this revelation strengthens, which it always does, you finally can see that all you really lost was a source of unconscious sorrow you'd always mistaken for being you! What a relief.

These discoveries deliver into your hands a personalized invitation to find what is your own free and fearless life. We can summarize our study to this point as follows:

On the other side of any conscious risk is the realization that who you really are has nothing to fear. But in order to make this self-liberating discovery, you must willingly face those fears, whatever they may be.

Here's some extra encouragement. The moment of real conscious risk always feels like a tunnel with no light at its other end. But each time you'll choose to enter it, that tunnel will turn into a bridge spanning the space between your past fearful life . . . and your new fearless one.

Choosing Your New Direction

Following are examples of everyday events, each of which presents a unique opportunity to take a conscious risk. And, as you'll see, even the most common occurrences hide within themselves secret bridges to new self-wisdom and greater inner strength.

1. Risk Saying No

The first step toward having your own free life begins with daring to refuse the silent demands of others. Saying "yes," for fear of saying "no" is a recipe for resentment. Risk walking away from fear. Say "no."

2. Risk Leaving Empty Spaces Empty

Giving yourself empty things to do can't fill that emptiness you feel inside. So risk leaving that space empty. Allow it to fill itself, which it wants to do, with something you can't give yourself: The end of feeling empty.

3. Risk Not Defending Yourself

It's only when you consciously risk laying down your armor, shield, and sword; your quips, retorts, and criticisms that you discover who you really are can't be hurt. Risk letting others win.

4. Risk Appearing Stupid

Pretending to understand something that you don't, for fear of appearing stupid, only ensures that you'll remain a fearful pretender for the rest of your life. And that's stupid. Risk asking all the questions you need to ask. That's smart!

5. Risk Bearing Your Own Burdens

The weight of any trouble is determined by how much you fear it. But the only weight any fear can have is what you give to it when you try to push it away. Risk not "sharing" your burdens. Stop pushing them onto others. You'll be amazed how light they really are.

6. Risk Being Rejected

"No" is just a word; the fear of it is a prophecy self-fulfilled. Be bold! Risk asking for what you really want. Reject the fear of being rejected by daring to say "no" to the fear of no.

7. Risk Catching Yourself in the Act

Your life can't be both a show and be real. Catch yourself in the middle of some self-created drama and just drop it. Risk bringing the curtain down on yourself. Life is real only when you are.

8. Risk Taking the Lead

You can never know the true pleasure and spiritual satisfaction of having your own life until you take the risk of finding it for yourself, all by yourself. Followers fear to tread that higher inner road called "My Own Way." Risk going out in front.

9. Risk Letting Go

You've been trying to run your own show and, so far, it's pretty much been a nightmare with entertaining intermissions! Risk letting something higher have its hand at directing your life. Let your show go.

10. Risk Being No One

Everyone wants to be seen by others as being great. This makes that kind of greatness common. Be awake to what is common in your life and then risk doing the opposite. Real greatness follows.

Your Higher Destiny

Look for your own moments where taking a conscious risk will lead you to a liberating self-discovery. Following is a helpful hint to get you started looking in the right inner direction.

In earlier times, prospectors searched for gold along riverbanks and in the exposed beds of mountain streams. Besides knowing how to look for the right geological formations, where it was likely gold nuggets lay hidden just under the sandy gravel, the best prospectors also had a special trick up their sleeve that helped shift the odds of finding gold in their favor.

As they walked along the water's edge, they placed themselves with the sun to their back and watched for a slight glint or golden flash in the sand. They knew from experience that where there were flakes of gold, there were also chunks. By following a similar approach in your search for inner gold, you can succeed in this exercise of taking conscious risks. Here's the parallel:

Watch yourself, all the time, wherever you are and whatever you may be doing. Watch for that telltale flash of resistance, anger, frustration, anxiety, or fear. Then let your heightened inner awareness lead you to the prize of self-liberation.

Since your usual reaction to any negative emotion is to avoid the condition or person you think is responsible for that feared feeling, your new and higher action is to consciously go toward that flash. In other words, don't walk away from what you see as being the source of your negative state; instead, willingly walk toward it, trembling if you have to!

Risk it! The priceless inner gold of a fearless life is waiting there just for you.

Special Summary

True strength is the flower of
wisdom, but its seed is action.

What did you do today to receive your instruction?

—Louis Pasteur

Chapter Seven

Step 3:
Cancel Self-Wrecking Resentments

Special Insight

WHATEVER FORM YOUR RESENTMENTS may take, they wreck only you . . . not the one you resent.

The Road Before You

Two men stroll down a leaf-covered wood lot path on a clear, brisk autumn morning. Jeff and Mark have been friends for years. They enjoy their Saturday morning walks and talks together. Yet, something's different about Mark today. Jeff senses there's a problem. But he says nothing.

Two minutes later, Mark stops walking and turns to Jeff. His eyes are searching for a place to begin. Then, following right behind his slowly spreading smile, these words spill out: "Jeff, are all these voices that are arguing in my head bothering you too?"

A second later, they both break out laughing. The spell Mark had been under was suddenly broken. He had been the captive of a dark inner dialogue.

What's a dark inner dialogue? Just what it sounds like: A negative tug-of-war in the unseen recesses of your mind where you're the only one pulling on both ends of the rope. Still more to the point, being in a dark inner dialogue is finding yourself losing a heated argument when there's no one else in the room with you!

What causes these dark inner dialogues? Resentment. So, here's a key thought to help you release this self-wrecking inner state: Holding onto some hurt or hatred—over what someone may have done to you in the past—makes you that person's slave in the here and now.

If you're tired of being a slave to a painful relationship out of your past, this study and step in how to release resentments is sure to bring welcome relief.

For this lesson to succeed in its intended purpose, it's important to understand that resentment is a bitter pill made up of two layers. The first layer is created by our refusal to be self-ruling; saying "yes" when we really want to say "no!" is one good example. Fawning before others for fear of their reprisal is another. Both weak actions breed resentment, because our wish to falsely accommodate compromises our natural need to be self-commanding.

The second layer is resentment's "active" ingredient, the psychological component that keeps it alive and unwell. This is the dark inner dialogue. These unconscious conflicts, in dialogue form, play themselves out in our mind by painfully reenacting various scenes from our past; moments gone by in which we either know, or sense, we were compromised by our own weakness.

And now comes another key thought.

If these inner dialogues were left to themselves as they popped into our mind, they'd be as powerless to disturb us as an echo is to change its own sound. Where we get into trouble, when resentment rules, is when we're unknowingly drawn into these scenes out of our past and find ourselves interacting with a cast of ghost players! The ensuing mental dialogue is always a desperate but futile attempt to change what has already been said and done so that maybe this time around we can come out a winner.

One good example of this kind of dark inner dialogue is giving someone a heated piece of your mind—when he or she is not around to hear it!

Choosing Your New Direction

Tired of going twelve rounds in routine fight scenes that always turn out the same?

Try this step for the winning solution.

If you sat down on a metal bench and suddenly realized the midday sun had heated it way beyond the comfort zone, you'd stand up as quickly as you could. The same intelligence behind this instinctive physical reaction can help you release all resentments and drop their dark inner dialogues.

Each time you catch yourself in a dark inner dialogue, of any kind, use your awareness of the conflict it's creating within you as a springboard to help you leap out of those scary scenes from your past into the safety of the present moment. Then, instead of giving yourself back over to those inner voices of conflict that are still trying to converse with you, remain aware of yourself in the present moment, and of their continuing beckoning presence.

No matter how many times you hear in your mind those fighting words that have always prompted you to jump into that dark dialogue, refuse to join in. Ground yourself in your awareness of the present moment.

Your Higher Destiny

The unconscious resentment responsible for creating heated scenes from the past cannot follow you into the now, which means no dark inner dialogue can tag along either. Why? Because when you're no longer a captive of your own past, you can recognize its ghost voices as the source of psychic intrusion they really are.

Remember, no dark inner dialogue can ever solve an unresolved resentment any more than one end of a snake is less the serpent.

Special Summary

Learn to ask for a happy, new
life by refusing to relive what's
been tearing at you.

Vengeance is mine, says the Lord.
—Old Testament

Chapter Eight

Step 4:
Step Out of the Rush

Special Insight

EVEN AT A MILLION MILES AN HOUR,
anxious thoughts and feelings still take
you nowhere.

The Road Before You

Before you can step out of the rush and
into your own life, you must first see
that while anxious, hurried feelings

often lend a temporary sense of self-importance, these same racing emotions actually rob you of the power you need to be self-commanding. A brief investigation will confirm this finding.

Self-command begins with being able to choose your own direction in life. And whether you're caught in the raging current of a white-water river, or being swept along by a flood of invisible thoughts and feelings, one fact remains: Like it or not, you're going where that current goes. You have no real choices as long as you're under its influence. That's why learning to step out of the rush is the same as learning how to step into your own life.

Allow the exercise described below to show you that your real nature never feels the need to rush any more than an eagle would try to swim across a lake to get to the other side.

Here's the challenge. Rushing thoughts and anxious feelings are invisible to you because each time they begin to race, you start to run with them. And after so many years of being carried along in this psychic slipstream, you've come to believe that either you are these surging inner currents or that their power is yours. Neither case is true. You are not these waves of thought any more than a cresting tide is the entire ocean.

instruction to help strengthen our resolve to stop this mad dash to nowhere: "Slow down. Relax. Dare to deliberately defy those inner screams that demand you rush nervously around. Instead, obey another quiet voice that assures you that the casual life is the truly powerful and efficient life."

Choosing Your New Direction

Beginning this very moment, intentionally separate yourself from any rushing inner condition by voluntarily stepping out of it. How can this be done? Purposefully slow yourself down by acting to consciously reduce your usual speed. Here are several suggested ways to guarantee a good start.

1. At fifty percent your normal gait, walk over to get your cup of coffee.

2. Try reaching for the phone, your glass of water or your pen at seventy-five percent your normal speed.

3. Drive the speed limit (at all times) but especially when late for an appointment.

One practice I find particularly profitable, at home and in business, is to pause a few seconds before I answer someone's question. This special conscious pause for self-awakening is invaluable because, as the old saying goes, "Only fools rush because, as the old saying goes, "Only fools rush in!" Whatever the occasion may be, choose the time and place to slow down, and then practice stepping out of the rush.

Your Higher Destiny

Here's the secret behind how this unique exercise delivers new self-command. Slowing down helps you become aware of yourself in a new and higher way by creating contrast between your usual speed through life and your now selectively slower one.

This enhanced self-awareness empowers you to step out of the rush of your own surging thoughts and feelings by making you conscious of their flooding presence within you as being something that doesn't belong to you. Once this is clear, then you can choose your own direction in life. Step out of the rush by slowing down. Do it now.

Special Summary

If you want to find what is timeless, dare to live as though you
have all the time in the world.

*Whoever is in a hurry shows that the
thing he is about is too big for him.*
—Philip Chesterfield

Chapter Nine

Step 5:
Refuse to Be
Self-Compromising

Special Insight

REFUSE TO COMPROMISE YOURSELF IN
the present moment for the promise of
a happier one to come.

The Road Before You

Your true nature is now. There is no
later. This means that before we can
change the unhappy endings in our
life, we must learn how to drop them

before they begin. And yes, this can be done. There is no other possible order; no other real correction for getting to the root of what's been wrecking our days.

The exercise described below has the power to change everything about your life for the better because it's all about changing how the troubling things in your life really begin. Your close study of these inner life lessons will reveal a hidden story. Watch how your new vision brings you new victory.

Choosing Your New Direction

The next time a want of any kind presses into your heart or mind, ask yourself these two questions: How do I feel about what I want? How does this want make me feel now?

For the best results, take a piece of paper and draw a line down the middle from top to bottom. At the top of the left-hand column, write the first question. At the top of the right-hand column, write the second question.

The first step is to notice the important difference between these two questions.

In the left-hand column, write down the thoughts and emotions that appear as you imagine how you're going to feel when you get the object of this new want. Perhaps you want a new job or higher position; a better relationship; a new outfit;

a vacation, or maybe that car you've been dreaming about driving across country.

What are some of the feelings that accompany such long-awaited wants? I'm sure you can list your own, but some examples include:

- excitement

- a sense of well-being

- the enjoyment of imagining yourself as the envy of all your friends

After taking inventory of how you think you're going to feel in that near or distant moment, take yourself out of this world of pleasing promises. Address the question in the right-hand column that asks you how this want makes you feel in the present moment.

Don't be concerned with what you may now discover within yourself. Just observe all those thoughts and feelings secretly attending to your want. Some of the surprising answers to "How does this want make me feel now?" could include feelings such as these:

- gripping anxiety

- disturbing or distant doubts

- worrisome fears

What exactly is happening here? Why do we find these negative states?

Follow closely: The same mind that projects a pleasure-to-come is instantly, but unconsciously, pained that it may not be able to possess that pleasure that it has imagined for itself. This invisible anguish is the root of self-compromise; for now we struggle to free ourselves from this self-created sorrow by doing "whatever it takes" to realize our wants.

Your Higher Destiny

If you work at this exercise and consciously apply its principles each time one of those familiar, haunting wants arises, you'll understand what few men and women have ever known: Each present moment is the seed of the next and it is the actual content of each successive present moment that brings us all that we experience as our life.

Your awakening awareness to what your wants are actually giving you will help you to change what you've been asking from life. And as your life-requests change in the now, in each present moment—from being secretly punishing to increasingly perceptive ones—you'll naturally begin to free yourself from all unconscious self-compromising acts.

Special Summary

You can't be divided and be content, so choose in favor of self-wholeness.

He who promises runs in debt.
>   —The Talmud

Chapter Ten

Step 6:
Take the Step that
You're Sure You Can't

Special Insight

EACH TIME YOU TAKE THE STEP THAT
you're sure you can't, you discover that
the "you" who would not was only a
thought that believed it could not.

The Road Before You

How many times have you found yourself thinking you'd like to develop a
new skill or sharpen an old one? Maybe

you've wanted to learn another language or play a musical instrument; further your education; or get up out of your easy chair and do some catch-up on that correspondence you've been putting off for weeks!

But in each, or at least most, of these instances, before you can even get started, you find yourself turned back—repelled from your upcoming chosen task by an onslaught of invisible forces! Suddenly, you're surrounded by deep weariness, self-doubt, mental fog, or sometimes just plain fear.

Do you recognize any of these self-stalling inner-attackers? Would you like to be liberated from their limiting influences? Freed to pursue higher levels of your own inner development? That's what this exercise is all about; teaching you how to take that next step each time you're sure you can't. Let's begin by covering a few basics in higher, or esoteric, psychology.

Most of us wouldn't be too surprised to hear that our mind has a will of its own. We all know what it's like to be more or less helplessly doing something we wish we weren't! We often feel the presence of this force within, but don't understand it—or its implications.

Figuratively speaking, every cell of your whole body has a "will" of a sort. This is a well-known scientific truth. Both the mind and the body are always hard at work, at a cellular level, to keep their lives—as they know them—in what is called "homeostasis." Don't let this strange-sounding term throw you. All it means is "the tendency of any organism, simple or complex, to want to maintain within itself relatively stable conditions." The translation as it concerns this exercise: There are more parts of you that want to stay the same than there are ones interested in growing or achieving new heights through effort.

The good news is that who you really are is greater than any one of these invisible aspects of yourself that are mechanically compelled to maintain its status quo. Your true nature is greater than the sum of all these physical, mental, and emotional parts. If you have any doubts about this, it's in your power to make this truth self-evident.

Choosing Your New Direction

The next time you want to go ahead with any project—whether it's designing a rocket ship or finally getting around to repairing your favorite rocking chair—and you start to feel those old familiar doubts, dreads, or doldrums rising up to block your way, just walk right through them. You can do it if you use your new wisdom to clear the way.

One excellent way to break through these seemingly impassable inner states is to see them as being the fakes they are. This isn't to say you won't feel their punishing presence when you first dare to defy their threats. But each time you psychologically walk up to and past these inner disturbances, you'll become increasingly aware that these task-resistant thoughts and feelings are just big fakes!

Your Higher Destiny

You must prove to yourself that these thoughts and feelings are fakes in order to know the powers that come with such a discovery. Following is a glimpse of what you'll learn each time you take that step you're sure you can't.

Those negative states that try to stop you from taking the next step of any chosen journey are just psychological special effects. These obstacles of psychic flash-and-smoke are generated by the mind to keep you from disturbing its established levels of comfort. But special effects, regardless of the kind of "screen" upon which they're projected, have no reality outside of your temporary belief in their appearance.

The truth is that these inner-barriers are without real substance, and so must vanish the moment you pass through them. Which brings us to a great spiritual truth; on the other side of the resistance is the flow. This means that each time you call on this exercise to walk through some pocket of inner resistance, you'll find, on its other side, all the fresh energy and intelligence you'll need to go through and complete your task.

All these years you've been taught to believe that before you can hope to succeed at something, you have to first feel as though you can. No! To succeed you need only understand how failure is created, and then consciously refuse to cooperate with what has been defeating you from within.

Special Summary

Each step into what you think you can't do is one step further away from that nature which wants you to think that circles actually go somewhere.

Every noble work is at first impossible.
—Thomas Carlyle

Chapter Eleven

Step 7:
Break Out of
the Blame Game

Special Insight

BLAMING CONFLICT-FILLED FEELINGS on any condition or person outside yourself is like getting angry at your shoes for being laced too tight.

The Road Before You

Most men and women recognize the need for a healthy balanced diet because good eating habits nourish the body. Good nutrition helps keep us agile and strong. And we also like to learn new skills to expand our interests. Challenging mental activities stimulate, sharpen, and strengthen the mind.

Now here's an effective inner life step designed to help you grow and develop greater spiritual strength: No matter what happens, never blame anyone—or anything—for the way you feel. Rising above the blame game is the same as learning how to be in total command of yourself.

Now comes an interesting surprise. In the step described below, it isn't what you do that contributes to your spiritual strength; it's what you don't do that bestows the greatest gain. And, as you'll learn, it's your aim not to blame that finally bestows the new strength you seek.

This approach to enhancing inner strength through quiet self-negation may seem confusing at first, so before we begin the hands-on part of this exercise, let's clear up any lingering questions you may have on the subject.

What Is Spiritual Strength?

Spiritual strength is many things that arise out of one. For the time being, following are three correct answers (the last one best serves our study together):

1. Spiritual strength is the power to live spontaneously free while remaining alert and fully
   responsible to the need of the present moment.

2. Spiritual strength is the courage to live
   exactly as you choose without the fear of
   being left out or of being left alone.

3. Spiritual strength is the higher understanding
   that gives you the power to not act from
   spiritual weakness.

What Is Spiritual Weakness?

Spiritual weakness is any unconscious aspect of
your nature that either causes you—or others—to
suffer. It is also anything that interferes with your
development of spiritual strength.

What's the connection between blaming others
for the way I feel and spiritual weakness?

Irritated inner states never seek solutions; they
only seek reasons for why they have a right to exist!
These states constantly feed you "good reasons" as
to why you feel badly. The weakness that blames
others blinds you to your real inner condition;
which is going nowhere except around and down.

Choosing Your New Direction

The next time you feel yourself starting to become frustrated, angry, or scared, do your best to confirm this next vital insight: Negative emotions cannot exist without having something to blame for their punishing presence.

The clearer for yourself you can make this spiritual fact—about the dualistic nature of spiritual weakness—the better prepared you'll be to take your next step toward higher spiritual strength. Your discovery leads you to this totally new action. Whatever it takes, don't express that surfacing irritation by naming or blaming anything outside of yourself as being its cause.

Even if you have to remove yourself physically from the developing situation, then do it. Find some way to temporarily isolate yourself—along with your smoldering emotional state. Please note: Isolate yourself along with your agitation.

Your Higher Destiny

If it helps to make what appears to be a bitter pill taste better, think of these inner trials as the pause that spiritually strengthens, for a new strength is exactly what you'll win for yourself each time you elect to work with this step.

Voluntarily isolating yourself along with your irritated thoughts and feelings doesn't mean cutting them off; nor does it mean that you should pretend that you're not on fire. Suppression of these weak inner states is just the opposite of angrily expressing them, and every bit as harmful. Don't express—or suppress—any negative state. Besides, either one of these opposite approaches always produces the same results; nothing changes except for what's being blamed. Choosing to not blame lifts you above both of these losing choices.

Your conscious non-action turns you into the objective witness of your own superheated emotions. And from the safety of this higher awareness you see about yourself what you couldn't see before because of all the inner fire and smoke. Your discoveries empower you to cancel the real cause of your inner combustibility. Not only is your self-command restored, but it's heightened. Each discovery of an unseen weakness heralds the coming of a greater spiritual strength.

Be sure to practice the pause that spiritually strengthens. Refuse to blame.

Special Summary

Choose to change right now, and you won't have to worry about how to be different next time.

The strength of a man sinks in the hour of trial: But there doth live a power that to the battle girdeth the weak.

—Joanna Baillie

Chapter Twelve

Step 8:
Erase Those
Fearful Feelings

Special Insight

THERE IS NO SUCH THING AS A SHAKY situation, so any time you start to tremble, don't look around you for the fault. Look inward. It is the inner ground you are standing on that is not solid.

The Road Before You

That seemingly scary condition, whatever it may be, is not the problem. It's your reaction that has you shaking. And that's why, if you'll become conscious of a fearful condition instead of afraid of it, you'll change forever your relationship with fear. It's true.

Being conscious of your fear empowers you to interact with it in an entirely new way. This new inner relationship gives you the power to be awake to your fear's scary influences, instead of being their unconscious slave. And as each day you discover something new about the shaky nature of your own fearful reactions, those reactions lose their power over you. Why? You see them for what they have always been; unintelligent, mechanical forces.

To be consciously afraid means that you know you are frightened, but at the same time, to know that these very fears, as real as they may seem, are not you.

Fear is really nothing other than a self-limiting reaction that we've always mistaken for a shield of self-protection. It's time to let it go, which you can do anytime you want. Here's how: Dare to proceed, even while being afraid.

Employing this simple but higher instruction to proceed even while being afraid will not only show you the strange faces of all those habitual reactions that have had you on the run, but it will also empower you to start seeing through them. And, as you'll gratefully discover, each of your new insights into their actual nature removes some of their power over you. Better yet, their loss is your gain! The following step will help you face those fearful feelings and erase them from your life once and for all.

Choosing Your New Direction

Do you know someone whom you would rather run from than run into? Most of us do! Nevertheless, starting right now, resolve never again to avoid any person who scares you. In fact, whether at home or work, go ahead and walk right up to that critical or aggressive person and say exactly what you want, instead of letting the fear tell you to do what it wants. Have no ideas at all about the way things should or shouldn't go. Of course, this exercise is not an excuse to be cruel or rude.

Remember, your aim in working with this step in self-liberation is not to win an ego victory, but rather to watch and learn something new about yourself. Drop any other misplaced self-conscious concerns. Let that person see you shake, if that's what starts to happen. What do you care? It's only temporary. Besides, that unpleasant person before you can't know it, but you're shaking yourself awake!

Stand your inner ground even if it feels as though you might fall through the floor. Allow your reactions to roll by you—instead of letting them carry you away as they've always done in the past.

Your Higher Destiny

If you'll fight for yourself in this new way, it won't be the floor beneath you that you feel open. It will be your inner eyes! And what they see is that this flood—of what were once unconscious reactions—has its own life story; a shaky story that up until now you'd taken as your own. But it's not. You see these fears don't belong to you, and that they never have. Everything about your life changes in this one moment. Here's what has been revealed to you:

You've never been afraid of another person. The only thing you've ever been frightened by is your own thoughts about that person. Yes, you did feel fear, but it wasn't yours. And it wasn't toward someone stronger than you. The fear you always felt was in what you thought he or she was thinking about you. Amazing isn't it? You have been afraid of your own thoughts.

Facing your fearful feelings brings them to an end because if you proceed while being afraid, you'll see all that has been scaring you . . . is you.

Special Summary

You only have to enter the fear of the unknown once, while you must live the fear of pretending you know with each pretense.

There is great beauty in going through life without anxiety or fear. Half our fears are baseless, and the other half discreditable.

—Christian Bovee

Chapter Thirteen

Step 9:
Release and
Relax Yourself

Special Insight

NATURAL AND UNRESTRICTED ENERGY
is to your health, happiness, and spiritual development as a snow-fed river is
to a high mountain lake; both must be
renewed each day.

The Road Before You

Most people spend much of their lives in
a constant struggle to hold themselves
together. Even a brief glance shows us

that a life spent in this futile fashion is most likely an unproductive one. The energies that are meant to be poured into creative expression and continued self-development are used instead to just keep common things in place. The following special exercise, one of my favorites, is all about letting yourself fall apart.

Please! Don't be put off by the mere mention of this unusual approach to physical and spiritual revitalization. Once you release the energies you have wasted in undetected physical tension, you can redirect them to supply you with an abundant source of inner peace, higher intuition, and an unshakable sense of well-being.

There really is a secret way to let yourself go that will, at the same time, get you going—and doing—and feeling better than you have in a long time. Read on!

Each day we are allotted a certain amount of life-energy. In the East this inner force is called *chi*; in India, *prana*. The name of these energies varies by culture, but not the fact of its existence. If you doubt this daily distribution of life-force, ask yourself the following three questions, and then seriously ponder their answers.

1. Where does the energy come from that's allowing you to hold this book—or to have the thoughts and feelings you're experiencing right now?

2. Are you the source of the life-force that beats your heart and empowers you to take that breath you just took?

3. Are you the creator of your own animating energy, or are you its creation?

The energy used to sustain our lives is given to us daily. But how those energies are used is given to us to decide. So this exercise is about making the conscious decision to relax and release yourself.

With conscious effort, you can learn to release those vital energies that are being wasted in undetected physical tension. What will liberating these natural forces do for you? Everything!

Imagine what happens to a flourishing orchard when the stream that naturally irrigates it is accidentally blocked or diverted by a large, fallen boulder. The orchard is able to continue living, but not nearly to its potential. Growth is stunted; life held back.

Now imagine that obstructing rock being removed. The waters return and with them the orchard's original vitality. New, vigorous growth is ensured.

Common physical tension is a boulder that blocks—and wastes—our overall energies. Poor health, irritated nerves, and vague anxieties are just a few of the ways blocked energies negatively impact our everyday lives.

Choosing Your New Direction

The following is a soothing and sound way to remove invisible inner rocks and realize refreshing new vitality. At least three times a day, decide to relax and release yourself. Use the technique that follows, but don't get tensed up trying to comply with a set of instructions.

Close your eyes and bring your attention to the top of your head. Become aware of your scalp area and those muscles that span across your forehead and temples. Allow them to relax. Give these muscles a quiet mental command to let go, and then let them do as you've asked. If necessary (and most likely it will be), repeat this silent release instruction and letting-go action several times until you feel a definite response. Don't get frustrated if at first you don't succeed. Your muscles have probably been tense for so long they may not know how to relax, let alone remain at ease in that state. Stick with it.

In a few moments, or however long it may take, when your muscles yield to your decision to relax, you'll feel a pleasant sensation ease down from the crown of your head and continue to move downward along its sides. Give your complete attention to the inviting movement of this spreading relaxation. Let yourself go with its gentle flow.

Now, while remaining aware of the forces you've set in motion, take the next step. Place your attention on the muscles all around—and particularly just beneath—your eyes.

There's a tremendous amount of tension stored in this facial muscle group. In fact, these muscles may be so rigid that, at first mental survey, this whole area may feel as though it's locked up, and unable to be released. Be patient with yourself, but persist. This stubborn tension will yield.

As these energies are released, you may feel some trembling or quivering in those areas; have no concern. In time, as you continue to refine this exercise and keep these muscles relaxed all day long, you'll feel your entire facial structure start to change. There's a good chance your eyesight could improve. Who knows? You might even get better looking!

Continue to relax and release yourself by applying the same procedures to the area around your mouth. Stay in conscious touch with yourself to see that all previously released muscle groups are remaining at ease. Now go ahead and relax the neck, shoulders, chest, arms, and hands. Use the same technique of focusing on a body part or muscle group and consciously deciding to relax that part of yourself.

If you want to, and if time permits, relax and release yourself in this way all the way down to your toes. If you have trouble falling asleep at night, this complete body release is especially helpful for inducing a deep relaxed state. You'll awaken more refreshed too.

Your Higher Destiny

Remember: Freedom is natural. While on the road to self-release, allow your natural interest and the inner discoveries it reveals to be your final guide.

When you first begin to practice this step, find a comfortable place where you can be alone. Before too long, however, you'll learn to apply this energy-releasing and life-renewing inner technique anywhere, anytime, and under any circumstances.

Eventually, after you get the feel for it, you'll be able to do this exercise with your eyes open.

It's always the right time to be relaxed. Create your own abbreviated form of these self-release techniques. Learn to release and relax yourself while you're on the phone, watching TV, or even when you're out dining with friends.

Special Summary

Every day: Casual, but industrious. Every moment: Relaxed, but alert.

If the mind, that rules the body, ever so far forgets itself as to trample on its slave, the slave is never generous enough to forgive the injury, but will rise and smite the oppressor.

—Henry Wadsworth Longfellow

Chapter Fourteen

Step 10:
Stop this Secret
Self-Sabotage

Special Insight
THERE IS NO PLEASING THE FEAR THAT
you may displease others.

The Road Before You
It's a little-known yet much denied fact
that people treat you the way you
secretly ask to be treated. Your unspo-
ken request that determines how others
behave toward you is extended to—and

received by—everyone you meet. This petition is broadcast, second by second, in the form of silent messages emanating from your own invisible inner life.

What is your invisible inner life? It's the way you actually feel—as opposed to the way you're trying to appear—when meeting any person or event.

In other words, your invisible inner life is your real inner condition. It's this state of internal affairs that communicates with others long before any words are exchanged. These silent signals from your inner self are what a person receives first upon meeting you. The reading of them determines, from that point forward, the basis of your relationship. This unseen dialogue that goes on behind the scenes whenever two or more people meet is commonly understood as "sizing one another up." But here's the point of this introduction.

We're often led to act against ourselves by an undetected weakness that goes before us—trying to pass itself off to others—as a strength. This is secret self-sabotage. It sinks us in our personal and business relationships as surely as a torpedo wrecks the ship it strikes. Learning how to stop this self-sinking is the focus of this exercise. Let's begin by gathering the higher insights we'll need to succeed.

Any person you feel the need to control or dominate—so that he or she will treat you as you "think" you should be treated—will always be in charge of you . . . and treat you accordingly. Why? Because anyone from whom you want something, psychologically speaking, is always in secret command of you. The dynamics of this spiritual law are revealed in the following paragraph.

It would never dawn on any person to want to be more powerful or superior to someone else unless there was some psychic character within him or her that secretly felt itself to be weaker or lesser than that other individual. From where else would such a petty concern originate if not out of an unseen, unsettling feeling of inferiority?

Genuine inner strength neither competes nor compares itself to others any more than an eagle wants to fly like a crow or waddle like a duck. Neither real strength nor regal eagle has any need to prove anything.

What this important lesson teaches us is that any action we take to appear strong before another person is actually read by that person as a weakness. If you doubt this finding, review the past interactions and results of your own relationships. The general rule of thumb is that the more you demand or crave the respect of others the less likely you are to receive it. If you've ever tried to raise children, you know this is true.

So it makes no sense to try and change the way others treat you by learning calculated behaviors or attitude techniques in order to appear in charge. The only thing these clever cover-ups really produce is yet another source of secret inner conflict, which, in turn, only fuels further self-sabotage. Besides, what you're really looking for in your relationships isn't command over others—but over yourself. So what's the answer?

Choosing Your New Direction

Stop trying to be strong. Instead, start catching yourself about to act from weakness.

Don't be too surprised by this unusual instruction. A brief examination reveals its wisdom. Following are ten examples of where you may be secretly sabotaging yourself while wrongly assuming you're strengthening your position with others.

1. Fawning before people to win their favor.

2. Expressing contrived concern for someone's well-being.

3. Making small talk to smooth out the rough edges.

4. Hanging onto someone's every word.

5. Looking for someone's approval.

6. Asking if someone is angry with you.

7. Fishing for a kind word.

8. Trying to impress someone.

9. Gossiping.

10. Explaining yourself to others.

Let's look at this last act of secret self-sabotage, explaining yourself to others, and use it to see how we can transform what has always been the seed of some self-sinking act into a conscious source of self-command.

The next time you feel as though you need to explain yourself to someone (other than to your employer as it may concern his or her business affairs), give yourself a quick and simple internal test. This test will help you check for and cancel any undetected weakness that's about to make you sabotage yourself.

Here's what to do: Run a pressure check.

Here's how:

Come wide awake and run a quick inner scan within yourself to see if that question you're about to answer—or that answer you're about to give, without having been asked for it—is something you really want to do. Or are you about to explain yourself because you're afraid of some as yet undisclosed consequence if you don't?

Your Higher Destiny

This self-administered test for inner pressure is how you tell if your forthcoming explanation is truly voluntary, or if you're on the verge of being shanghaied into an unconscious act of self-sabotage. Your awareness of any pressure building within you is proof that it's some form of fear—and not you— that wants to do the explaining, fawning, impressing, blabbing, or whatever the self-sabotaging act the inner pressure is pushing you to commit.

Each time you feel this pressurized urge to give yourself away, silently but solidly refuse to release this pressure by giving in to its demands. It may help you to succeed sooner if you know that fear has no voice unless it tricks you into giving it one. So stay silent. Your conscious silence stops self-sabotage.

Special Summary

In any and every given moment of your life, you are either in command of yourself . . . or you are being commanded.

In all our weaknesses we have one element of strength if we recognize it. Here, as in other things, knowledge of danger is often the best means of safety.

—E. P. Roe

Chapter Fifteen

Step 11:
Go Quiet

Special Insight

THE FRANTIC SEARCH FOR ANY ANSWER only delivers answers on the same frantic level.

The Road Before You

One of the most powerful forces in the universe available to human beings is also one of the least understood and appreciated. The subject of this step is silence.

The wise words of Richard Cecil, an eighteenth-century English author and theologian, set the stage for our study:

> The grandest operations, both in nature and grace, are the most silent and imperceptible. The shallow brook babbles in its passage and is heard by everyone; but the coming of the seasons is silent and unseen. The storm rages and alarms, but its fury is soon exhausted, and its effects are but partial and soon remedied; but th dew, though gentle and unheard, is immense in quantity, and is the very life of large portions of the earth. And these are pictures of the operations of grace in the church and in the soul.
>
> But don't be mislead. Reach no conclusions about the true nature of what is quiet. The secret strength of silence can be as practical in your everyday life as is its real character to be life changing. You can actually have—and benefit directly from—a quiet mind.

To help bring this important and higher self-possibility down to earth, I've prepared a list of twenty-five powers that can be directly attributed to a mind that has found real silence. Be amazed! And then take action. The exercise that follows this list places you on the inner road that leads to the source of these true strengths.

A quiet mind . . .

1. Is spontaneously creative in any situation.

2. Can neither betray itself nor anyone else.

3. Rests naturally when it isn't naturally active.

4. Knows without thinking.

5. Seeks nothing outside of itself for strength.

6. Detects and easily rejects psychic intruders.

7. Never compromises itself.

8. Can't be flattered or tempted.

9. Doesn't waste valuable energy.

10. Fears nothing.

11. Can't outsmart itself.

12. Is never the victim of its own momentum.

13. Refreshes itself.

14. Is in relationship with a higher intelligence.

15. Never struggles with painful thoughts.

16. Is instantly intuitive.

17. Gives its undivided attention to its tasks.

18. Receives perfect direction from within.

19. Deeply enjoys the delight of its own quietness.

20. Lives above expectations and disappointments.

21. Can't be captured by regrets.

22. Commands every event it meets.

23. Lives in a state of grace.

24. Never feels lonely.

25. Knows and helps quietly design its destiny.

When you want to directly enjoy the sunshine, you must go outdoors. You understand you have to take yourself physically to a place where the warming rays of the sun can fall upon you without interference. Likewise, when you want to know the powers that circulate through a quiet mind, you must take yourself to that place where this silent strength can make itself known to you. To go quiet, you must go within.

In those days now past, when Christ told his disciples to seek the Kingdom of Heaven within, his words of wisdom were not the religion they've become today. They were alive with secret but ever-so-practical instructions on how a person could discover and realize a secret part of himself or herself that was not a part of what was then—and of what still remains—a conflict-torn and weary world.

This master instruction still holds true. If we want to know that stillness, that silent strength, a peace that passes all understanding, we must go within. We must go quiet.

Choosing Your New Direction

The best time to practice going quiet is when the world around you is already in a natural state of silence. Early morning, upon arising, and just before you go to sleep are the most likely times to yield the best results. But as you'll no doubt come to discover for yourself, anytime is the right time to go quiet.

Find a place to sit, such as a comfortable chair, where your back can be supported and held straight. Let your hands rest, open or closed, in any position that won't cause tension to themselves, your arms, or shoulders. Remain seated for the duration of your practice. Twenty to thirty minutes twice a day is a suggested minimum time to sit quietly. But do the best you can. There are no laws that govern inner silence. Besides, the day may come when you'd like to sit for longer durations, so you be the judge. Let the length of this time for inner quiet be whatever it wants to be.

Allow your legs to assume whatever position is most naturally relaxed for them. It's better if you don't cross your legs one over the other as this posture interferes with your circulation and the ensuing discomfort will become a distraction.

Once your body is situated and in relative ease, close your eyes and let your awareness sweep over the whole of your body. (To enhance the benefits of this exercise, use the practices found in Step 9, "Release and Relax Yourself.") Adjust your limbs again, if necessary, so that no individual part of your physical self is calling out for your attention.

Now, with your eyes still gently closed, let your shoulders take the full weight of your head. You should actually be able to feel the physical transfer of this weight take place.

Then give the weight of your shoulders and your arms to the armrests of your chair, or to whatever part of your body is beneath them. If you're doing this properly, you'll be surprised how much of your own bodily weight you were unnecessarily supporting without knowing it!

Finally, give all this collective weight—head, shoulders, arms, upper body, buttocks, and legs—to the chair or sofa you're sitting upon. Consciously transfer the weight. Let it go. Then let yourself sink into the feeling that comes with releasing all this unconscious physical stress and tension.

The next step is to continue expanding this relaxed and increased awareness of your body to include within it the awareness of your thoughts and feelings. In other words, bring into your enhanced physical awareness the further awareness of what your mind and emotions are doing in the moment. You watch yourself.

Your Higher Destiny

This form of self-observation is as interesting as it is challenging. To ensure your success in this going within and going quiet, consider yourself as being a naturalist of the mind.

A good wildlife naturalist casually observes the diverse ways of birds or bunnies without interfering. In order to study and learn, he or she just watches. And that's what you must learn to do as you journey within. You're to be an impartial witness to the life of your own thoughts and feelings. Let them fly and hop around within you without the slightest concern for their direction or character. Neither resist nor let yourself be drawn into any of their attention-stealing antics.

Again, all you want to do is watch. Detached self-observation is your aim. Each time you realize that you're no longer watching, but rather that you've been captured by a thought or feeling and are being carried along by it, just quietly withdraw yourself from that temporary psychic wave. Come back to the awareness of yourself in the present moment.

This part of your practice is the heart and soul of going—and knowing—quiet. You must experience it for yourself. As you sit, let go, give up, go within, and watch. And over and over again, bring your awareness of yourself back into the awareness of the present moment.

One special way to help "ground" yourself in the now is to use your awareness of each out-breath as a reminder to give all your weight back to the chair. Each time you breathe out, let yourself go completely. Stay watchful and consciously drop the heaviness of your body, mind, and emotions. Let something else be responsible for their weight. This is the greatest feeling in the world, and it prepares you for the eventual higher stages of this exercise.

Pay no attention to what your own thoughts and feelings are trying to tell you the whole time you're sitting, which is namely this: "You should give up this worthless, unproductive practice!"

Learn to watch and drop these dark inner voices. They don't want you to succeed and there's a good reason why. They can't dwell in that silent world you wish to enter and that wishes to enter you.

So persist! You will prevail. For even as you struggle to stay aware of yourself in the present moment, that moment itself changes. And as it does, so do you.

Slowly, subtly at first, but eventually even beyond your mind's protests, the distinction between your sense of self and your awareness of the present moment melts away. And as it does, a new, deeper sense of silence floods into you; filling your awareness with itself and, at the same time, with yet another awareness that the source of this supreme stillness is arising out of your own being. It washes everything out of its way. And so arrives a quiet mind.

Special Summary
Just as you can see farther on a clear day, new understanding flowers in a quiet mind.

The sovereignty of nature has been allotted to the silent forces. The moon makes not the faintest echo of a noise, yet it draws millions of tons of tidal waters to and fro at its biding. We do not hear the sun rise, nor the planets set. So, too, the dawning of the greatest moment in a man's life comes quietly, with none to herald it to the world. In that Stillness alone is born the knowledge of the Overself. The gliding of the mind's boat into the lagoon of the spirit is the gentlest thing I know; it is more hushed than the fall of eventide.

—Dr. Paul Brunton

PART THREE

*Success Through
Higher Self-Studies*

Chapter Sixteen

Step 12:
5 Practices to Complete Freedom from Stress

Special Insight

FREEDOM FROM THE PRISON OF THOUGHT begins with being free to think, and you cannot freely consider your own condition if you have a vested interest in remaining you.

The Road Before You

The intention of this chapter is to place into your mind, heart, and hands a powerful and new inner life step. Prior to the explanation of this master step, we'll explore and expand upon what has been the real lesson hidden at the root of all the exercises given in this book.

Don't be too concerned if you have some initial difficulty seeing (during your first or second reading of this chapter) how this new information unites the lessons of your earlier studies. For one thing, you'll need to work with all of these exercises for some time before you're able to see how all the various states of spiritual sleep are related in the way they wreck happiness, just as how all principles and forces of the awakened life work together for your true and lasting contentment.

Be patient with yourself, but don't pamper yourself either. This chapter is the most challenging in the book, but it also reveals, clearly, the core of not only what has been running you around in stressful circles, but the foundation of a whole new order of higher personal freedom.

To be human is to long for complete self-liberty. In one sense we get stressed-out not so much by unwanted events themselves, but by the fact that each of these disconcerting moments shows us we've yet to find the way to the contented life our hearts long for.

Something else that we all share in common is that we know our true destiny is not of this earth; that we are, somehow, made of finer stuff. Well and true—we should reach for the stars. But while we do, let us not forget that these seemingly distant heavens must dwell somewhere within the present ground of ourselves; that it is here we must each begin digging and into which we must sow the seeds of truthful principles . . . such as the ones revealed in the following short story.

Paul had reached the end of his rope. With over half of his cruise ship vacation ruined by a strange seasickness, he'd clearly run out of options. Not only had the ship enjoyed calm seas, but he'd never had this problem before! Besides, below in his cabin he felt fine, great in fact. It was only when he ventured up on deck that the dreaded queasiness crept in.

So, feeling fine, again, on the morning of the fourth day, he dressed himself in his shipboard's finest, donned his new sunglasses, and headed toward the upper viewing deck. But within five minutes of sitting down, he was up and standing over the rail, taking in deep breaths of cool air to calm his rolling stomach. It was just then that the captain of the ship walked over to him, and both men stood there looking out at the bright, open seas. After a moment, the captain spoke.

"Not feeling too well it seems?"

A little embarrassed, Paul hesitated before speaking. "I'm not exactly on the top of my game, but thanks for asking."

Another pause and the captain turned to face Paul's side. "I think I might know what's wrong."

Paul thought to himself, in a definite sarcastic tone, "Gee, really!" but said instead, "Oh? And what's that?"

The captain knew he was on sensitive ground by the tone of Paul's voice, and so he stepped back a half-foot before answering him. "Do you mind if we try a small experiment that may help you feel a lot better?"

Paul turned to face him, mustering up a half smile. "Sure, I don't see why not. I've tried everything else. What did you have in mind?" And before he knew it, the captain had reached over and gently slid Paul's new aviator glasses off his face.

"What's the deal?" he said, slightly squinting his eyes in the bright morning light.

"Just wait a few minutes," the captain answered. "You'll see."

The two of them stood there with only the sounds of the ship cutting her way through the waters beneath them. What seemed too many minutes later, about the same time he was getting past how uncomfortable he felt standing there saying nothing, Paul noticed something else was disappearing—his seasickness!

A bit stunned, and almost reluctant to say anything for fear of wrecking his good fortune, he spoke up.

"I can't believe it," he said, as he inventoried himself once more, just to be sure, "but I do feel better." And he looked into the captain's eyes for an explanation of some kind.

The captain spoke as he handed Paul back his sunglasses, but his explanation came as a complete surprise.

"It's so simple as to not be believable, but I've seen this a few times before. That's how I knew. Only I just couldn't be sure without a small test."

"What could he be leading up to?" Paul wondered, but he held himself back from speaking aloud, which permitted the captain to continue uninterrupted.

"I suspected that the real reason you didn't feel well had to do with the light green tint of the lenses in your glasses—so that each time you came out on deck you saw everyone on it with a slight green cast to the color of their skin." The captain paused. "Then, your mind seeing everyone else as being seasick, well . . . it just started you feeling that way too." And he raised his eyebrows as if to say, "Amazing, isn't it?"

Paul's astonishment left him speechless, so the captain covered the moment for him. "Anyway," the captain said as he smiled a polite departing smile, "let me know if there's anything else I can do for you to make your voyage a pleasant one." And with that, as quickly as he'd appeared at Paul's side earlier that morning, he was gone. Paul enjoyed the rest of his travels without any problems.

Why Real Relief Must Include Self-Release

Here's the first important lesson in this simple story: Our experience of life is determined by how we see it. And how we see life is determined, each moment, by what we are looking at it through.

There are many times when we believe we see the world aright, but fail to see, as Paul was amazed to discover, that our view of the world has been colored; compromised, without our knowing it.

In Paul's case, what he couldn't see is that the very thing he was using to see his world through—his green-tinted lenses—was one of the conspirators in creating his sickness. Once the captain was able to show him the actual cause of his unhappy condition, his condition changed instantly. So, to help clarify one last important point, let's put ourselves in Paul's place for a moment to see what else we can learn from it.

Imagine all the steps Paul must have taken during those first three-and-a-half days in his search for some relief from feeling seasick: Drugs, naps, special foods, exercises, affirmations, and possibly prayers; perhaps he even spent precious energies resenting some friend of his who had urged him on a luxury cruise to "get some much needed rest and relaxation." Right!

Here's the point: Nothing Paul could have turned to for relief had a chance of working for him because—as the good captain's intervention revealed—what Paul really needed was to be released from his *misperception*, not relieved of the symptoms that it was causing.

Please take a moment here to consider this critical difference between searching for relief from some persistent trouble and being altogether released from it. Relief from something means its essential cause remains intact, even if temporarily abated. To be released from any problem you face is to resolve both its effects and cause.

We find it natural to seek relief from the world around us, a world appearing to be one stronghold atop another of stressful conditions and anxiety-producing events. Accordingly, we seek relief from these contentment-crushing states by struggling to change those circumstances we see as being responsible for their cause.

Think of all the ways we've attempted to escape those unwanted pressures we find ourselves feeling. But experience tells another story. The more we struggle to change or escape these stressful states of ours, the only thing that really seems to change is the "new" conditions we now see as being the cause of our stress! And it must continue in this way until we realize the truth of one central idea; a realization that leads to our release: What we actually need is not new forms of relief (from these perceived stressful places in our lives) but to be released from our own unconscious nature that is secretly creating the stress we've been blaming on situations outside of ourselves.

Let's examine this inner discovery using different terms. Stress, and all of its negative relatives, including impatience, anxiety, frustration, and anger, are the self-wrecking effects of first seeing, and then embracing, a false or incomplete view of reality imposed upon us by our own unenlightened nature.

The good news is that the stress-producing self that thrives in this inner shadowland disappears when the lights come on. And this is precisely our task, to bring much-needed Light into our developing consciousness. As we do, all of the conflict-creating creatures hiding therein have no choice but to depart. Inner victory comes in proportion to the amount of inner Light brought to bear. And since there's no end to this healing Light, there's no end to how bright—and free—our destiny can be. It will help if we pause here to summarize our findings up to this point.

The basic core of all true spiritual teachings is that the inner determines the outer. What this timeless idea means to us, relative to this chapter's lesson, is that what we receive from life—our experience of self in life—is determined by how we perceive events. And lastly, that how we perceive these life-moments is a creation of which parts of ourselves we see these same moments through.

A simple example of this internal dynamic, and how it colors our world, is seen in those moments when we're in a dark state of mind. No matter how bright the day, all we see around us is gloom and doom. That's why until we realize this inner relationship between those parts of ourselves perceiving life and our experience as a result of their unconscious interplay, we'll just keep seeing our stressful condition as something brought to bear upon us by a dark and uncaring world.

Wake Up and Break Up The Stress Cycle

What's required of us is a whole new self-understanding. We must learn what it means to reach for a whole new place within ourselves; to find and stand upon a higher ground from where it's possible to see that our present thoughts and feelings reveal only a fraction of the whole of our possible experience—instead of being what now defines our whole world for us through their conditioned and incomplete perception of it.

Reversing this unconscious condition in ourselves is both the purpose and the plan of the timeless truth. Insights and higher knowledge are its tools.

Our task is to be receptive and willing; to be open to what is trying to reach us and teach us about the truth of ourselves, and to accept the inner responsibility these timeless lessons reveal as being good and necessary for our freedom. As this higher receptivity and responsibility are united within us, a new destiny is forged for us. Its direction becomes one great power headed upward! Now let's learn how we might bring this power's promise to bear in our individual lives.

Have you ever heard yourself say, "What in the name of heaven was that all about?" and you were asking yourself what you had just done? Or along the same lines, "What on earth was I thinking?" when it became clear you weren't thinking at all! Then there's always, "How could I have been so stupid? So blind?" or . . . you fill in the blanks.

It's more than clear there are many times when we act out behaviors that, while seeming right to us at the time, are later found to be all wrong for us and everyone else unfortunate enough to have been caught up in our misguided choices. But how do such blunders take place, knowing that no one would consciously choose to defeat himself?

The simple answer is that we don't see what's actually before us. We are temporarily blinded, but not in the sense of having no vision. Our momentary blindness is to our own conditioned nature as it supplies us with its view of reality, one that we mistakenly accept as being ours; an error that can only be corrected by becoming more and more aware of the actual nature of our own internal workings. To see where we have been deceived, after the fall, is one thing. But learning to see how we're being fooled, right in the act of it, brings an end to both the fool and the fall brought on by his foolishness.

Following are five terms that describe five special principles, each of which will play a special role in our search into the real cause of stress. But don't permit yourself to become stressed over what these "terms" mean in and of themselves. Instead, allow me to show you how the operation of these five naturally occurring principles come to work together within you—to fuel each other—until their collusion causes you to see an unreal view of life; a false view that serves to supplant what is actual, and that leaves you struggling to deal with its unreal perception of life.

As we reveal the hidden internal operations of these five principles, you'll discover how all stressful, fearful, and anxious states are nothing more than the effect of unchecked thoughts and feelings being run through an unseen cycle. From these valuable insights you'll see how these five forces, and their presently undetected rela-tionships, conspire to color your perception, create stress, and rob you of your right to be self-determining. Then, just as promised in Christ's words, "Know the Truth and the Truth shall set you free," you'll discover how this new self-seeing is, indeed, the path to complete self-freeing.

The Attraction Principle

To begin with, it might be helpful to visualize how a landslide gets under way. Imagining this for a moment will prove valuable because just as there is always one movement, or suddenly loosed rock, that sets a mountainside into motion, so too is there always one definitive moment that starts the stress ball rolling. This moment that signals the onset of our stress, along with the cascading self-conflict it causes, operates under the law of attraction. To give ourselves a good idea of how these invisible laws of attraction work, both around and within us, let's look first at their more common expression in our natural world.

Just as the earth's gravity keeps us from floating off into space, the attractive power of the moon, its own gravity, pulls on our oceans producing what we know as tides. We can't see these forces themselves, but we are witnesses to their effects. Likewise, we know that the dolphin is attracted to the open seas, as surely as we can see how a moth is drawn to circle the light. And just as it's observably true that "birds of a feather flock together," or that we do tend "to assemble with those we resemble," these same laws of attraction apply to the more subtle worlds within us. Here their invisible influences operate tirelessly in the unseen regions of our mental and emotional lives, conducting our movements as surely as two magnets are either drawn to one another or repelled from each other depending upon which ways their poles are facing.

It will be helpful for your study of this principle if you consider, for a moment, how these forces of attraction influence your ways and days. Aren't some of us attracted to lose ourselves in the starry endlessness of a clear summer's night sky? Still others are drawn to gaze for hours on end into the flames of a campfire or winter's-night fireplace. And then there are those parts of people that are fascinated by disasters; that by a strange attraction are drawn to dwell upon global or personal tragedies that, as inescapable for them as is the moon from the earth's gravitational forces, holds them in their horrible wake. These small examples reveal one level of the law of attraction at work in our lives.

Let's delve deeper. In the still uncharted realms of mind and heart, there exist parts within every person that are drawn to seek out relationships with thoughts that are self-wrecking. For instance, we can often become transfixed by our own troubles, turning the image of some fear-producing picture over and over in our mind. And who hasn't found himself drawn into an argument where the antagonistic voice in his head is nothing other than his very own thoughts acting out the role of his enemy!

As these particular "birds of a feather"—these self-victimizing thoughts and feelings "flock together" in the unaware mind—this continual process (driven along by the law of attraction) eventually gives shape to a form of a psychic pathway; a kind of mental rut that ultimately expresses itself like this: In any psychologically challenging moment not only is the direction we turn to meet it already carved out for us, but what we meet that moment with, i.e., which parts of ourselves take the lead, is also reached automatically. So, in a very real sense, our choices are made for us even before we know what they are!

Have you seen this condition in yourself? That in a given "unwanted" event, because of some unpleasant past personal experience with others like it, a certain part of yourself rushes to the front and assumes command? In short, first these reactions define the moment and then rule the direction of all those that follow in its breaking wake.

For example, maybe someone makes a cutting remark towards you, or some pending news comes along concerning a possible loss of one nature or another. Doesn't it feel in these unwanted moments as though you're suddenly caught in a kind of gravitational field, as if something is literally pulling on you, within you, compelling you to seek out that part of yourself best able to consider your new condition? It is this exact inner moment, operating under the law of attraction, that is the real event responsible for the onset of your stressed states.

In and of themselves, our "scary" life-moments are as powerless to punish us as is a make-believe monster on the movie screen. For just as we must "give" ourselves over to the reality of the motion picture before we feel the fear it intends to raise in us, the same provisos hold true when it comes to our stressed moments. Before these familiar shakings and their aching can begin we must somehow be tricked into believing that what we're being given to see as the reality of our lives is, indeed, all there is to see about our real lives in that moment, which brings us to the study of our second stress-producing principle.

The Separation Principle

In our first look into the Attraction Principle we see how we can get drawn into, and begin dwelling within, what would be the otherwise passing world of some event. We've also touched upon how the degree of our identification with this same moment is strictly a condition of our individual past, and how this psychological body of our past experiences tends to be drawn to any such moment in which it recognizes something of itself. It's this internal process of attraction that sets the stage for the next phase of our study.

The Separation Principle operates in us in this way: *One passing event becomes our whole world.*

Please keep in mind throughout this investigation that each of the five principles to which you'll be introduced picks up where the one before it leaves off; working in a kind of alliance not unlike how adding one frame after another to a film further enhances its efficacy to sell that illusion it's produced to create. With this in mind, let's return to one of our earlier examples, where perhaps someone says something unkind to you.

The effect of the Separation Principle is to transform truly small moments into monstrous ones wherein all sense of proportion is lost. In no time at all the traditional "molehill" turns into the towering mountain. The outcome is inevitable: For the self drawn into it, nothing else matters or even exists. And as this event becomes ever enlarged in the mind, so is our attention increasingly drawn to its consideration; a condition of thought that not only effectively obscures the rescuing entrance of any other reality, but one which makes it appear that there is no other one.

At this stage our stress begins a steady escalation, because the more the mind struggles to release itself from its own unhappy condition, the more it looks to its own perception of the event for why it's in that event. The circle of self is closed. And it's right about here, psychologically speaking, that the third principle readies itself to enter into the fray.

The Isolation Principle

This third, and next stress-producing phase of the five principles in our study, works along similar lines as its immediate predecessor, only it operates in a different scale.

Just as the Separation Principle works by taking one passing event and, enlarging it until it effectively becomes the whole world for the one involved with it, the internal action of the Isolation Principle is to take this same narrowing of reality one step farther.

During this stage of the stress cycle the same unconscious forces of thought responsible for blowing everything out of proportion in its earlier incarnation, now begins to isolate or "spotlight" one particular feature within the reduced reality now perceived as being our entire world. A quick return to our running example of the instance where someone says something hurtful to us will best tell how this next stage serves to strengthen our growing misperception.

It's usually less than a matter of moments after that cruel comment comes crashing in on us that we start a certain kind of internal simmering. Our heated thoughts range from stewing over the nature of this "pathetic excuse for a human-being" that had the audacity to affront us, to how he or she hasn't one redeeming feature, and never has. And in the midst of this unconscious considering we begin to have what feels like 20-20 hindsight. Now, within what feels like our heightened scrutiny, we're able to see this person as having always been against us. And from this secretly self-punishing perception it's but a small step to take to begin berating ourselves for having been so blind!

And so it goes, bit by bit, slowly speeding up, these self-protecting thoughts continue to narrow down their consideration of the situation through their view of it. This focus soon finds its way to a kind of bizarre meditation upon one negative characteristic of the offending person and, in no time, this one questionable feature of his has become—to us—the very foundation of his being and of our justification for the war now raging within us. But there's more.

Now begins the second to the last stage of this unseen stress cycle; the proverbial icing on the cake that effectively convinces us that not only is our view of this emerging reality a clear and true one, but given this unwanted circumstance, we are more than entitled to believe in all the stressful states attending it! Let's look now at how our original "molehill" gets further transformed from being one imagined mountain into the entire range of the Rockies.

The Amplification Principle

To amplify is to increase, but in this study of the mechanism of stress we are discovering that the only thing truly being enlarged in these circumstances is our misperception of the event. Add to this mistaken view our subsequent certainty that we are also a captive of it, and our stress strengthens exponentially.

If you've ever looked through a pair of binoculars backwards then you have a good idea of how limiting and restrictive such a small focus on something can be. Where ordinarily we would look out and be able to see a vast forest, all we can see now is a small part of one tree. The same effect occurs within us as thought isolates the partial from the whole, so that now one small slice of reality is all the viewer sees. This is how the thought-self completes the deception. To us, as we find ourselves ever deeper in considering the circumstances surrounding the cruel remark, it actually seems as though our view is ever widening. But here's the truth: Our view is not truly enlarging. What is being enlarged, however, are all the ingredients the thought-self requires to justify the increasing levels of stress being brought to bear within us. Follow the steps:

First came the so-called disturbance; that cruel remark made by some thoughtless person, or news of whatever nature it takes to "shake" us up. In less than an instant, what is essentially a passing, neutral-by-nature moment becomes the center of our universe. Why? We're drawn into it.

As we're taken up into thinking over what's "at stake," our former view—of a once wider, more objective world—is replaced by the fully subjective world of what our anxious thoughts now see as being real. And with this first separation accomplished, our reality now changes with our every consideration of it. Please pause here to consider the implications of such a psychological condition. Let me restate it: What we now see before us as being real is only what we think we see.

We're almost entirely isolated from any possibility of rescuing reality at this point; a psychological condition just about impossible under "normal" circumstances as illusions (of any kind) can't maintain themselves through time without outside assistance. And there's no doubt that the inner deception responsible for our sense of stress would soon fall away were it not for the Amplification Principle kicking into gear.

In order to sustain this entirely false view of life, and to keep it from crumbling (which any illusion must do in the face of what's true), the thought-self must contrive a foundation to support its imagined conclusions. So, it begins building a case for itself to stand upon. For instance, it's suddenly able to recollect everything this troubling person ever did that ever troubled you at anytime, anywhere, in your history with him!

At this point there's nothing about the character of the offender too inane to deliberate about, no blemish too small, no past minor infraction that doesn't fit perfectly into the fractured view of the thought-self doing the reflecting. And as the case being built against the person reaches completion, all we're able to "see" is how justified we are in both our judgment of him, and for the unbearable stress we must endure until the situation is resolved.

The circle of stress drives itself from here on out. No other facts exist, and no interference is tolerated by anyone who would try and help us to wake up to reality. We believe we're alone, or certainly no one else quite sees the thing in the same clear light as we do. And to support this delusion the same nature that created and drew us into its ever-shrinking world has one more trick up its dark sleeve.

The Machination Principle

With our attention locked onto one small thing—and subsequently seeing our lives through this psychic pinhole—everything in our lives for that time period, be it a day or decade, serves to feed this false view and the stress it creates within us.

Haven't you seen this principle at work in yourself or others? It doesn't matter what comes along. Whatever, or whomever, it may be, is drawn into your stressed state where it's seen as being (at least) partially responsible for why you're in such pain. Even your overheating toaster oven becomes a part of the conspiracy against your happiness. This runaway-thought nature is like a tornado, drawing all moments into its winds; whirling thoughts that not only create the storm, but that continue to feed it as well.

So there you have the five principles responsible for the creation and continuation of the circle of stress:

> Attraction
>
> Separation
>
> Isolation
>
> Amplification
>
> Machination

Look closely at the first letter of each of these principles. Write them down on a sheet of paper if that's helpful to you.

What do these five letters spell out? ASIAM.

Now separate these five letters into three groups like this: As I Am. Remember this short phrase. It's an acronym for the five inner principles responsible for all stress and anxiety. With it to remind you, in your moment of need, of what you now know to be true about the actual nature of your stressed states, you can begin to break free of the circle of self and its falsehood. You can end its tyranny over you. I assure you this is possible; and even more.

Not only can you learn to drop those aches accompanying any stressful state, but as you do, you can be forever free of looking for things to blame for these pained feelings. You simply won't have these negative feelings any more!

Of course, best of all is not to fall into a stressed state to begin with. Wouldn't that be nice? Not only is such a self-composed life possible, but you may be assured that if you work to stay inwardly awake and aware of how these stressful states take their shape within you, this stress-less life will be yours. And just for the record, stress-less living means more energy, higher creativity, richer relationships, deeper compassion, less doubt, fear and confusion, and a finer, virtually unshakable sense of personal fulfillment. In short, real success without stress.

This state of true self-harmony is our aim. But lasting inner peace does not appear by itself. The stress-less life we long for is the marriage of new self-knowledge coupled with our willingness to act upon what we know as true. And this is where we must begin; within what we presently are, not in the hope of freedom as we imagine it, but in deliberate acts of freeing ourselves from what we can see within ourselves as self-sabotaging states.

Start this very moment putting into practice the new understanding you've already gained from your studies so far. With sincere effort on your part, not only can you learn how to detect the onset of any stressful thought or feeling, but you can discover the secret of how to use these self-defeating forces themselves to step out of their world and into a higher reality within which no stress can ever appear. You can do this.

Step Outside the Circle of Stress

At first glance, it appears these stressed sensations are there within you because of something "gone wrong" outside of you. But remember: This view of life belongs to the stressed self through whose eyes you are now looking at this event. So now is the time to shake yourself awake! What does this mean?

Understand the actual nature of the pressure within you. Instead of blindly seeing and accepting what your thoughts are describing to you as the "truth" of this moment, use your awareness of these anxious or stressed thoughts to come awake and to see these thoughts for what they really are. Each time you take this new inner action you will discover this amazing truth: You're not a captive of some stress-producing condition taking place somewhere outside of yourself. The truth is, in this moment, you are actually surrounded by an invisible circle of thoughts and feelings, all of which are pushing and pressing up against you to get you to acknowledge their reality. Why do they want your acknowledgment? Because your acceptance of their stressful nature within you unconsciously validates their reason for existing; reasons which, in turn, empower these same thoughts to tell you what to do about the stress you're starting to become aware of within yourself.

What should you do when finding yourself surrounded in this way? When perhaps you've already started sinking into a stressful state? See how evident the next step is; how simple and direct is the following solution to any developing stress once you know the truth as to its actual cause.

Step outside of the circle of stress. Deliberately take yourself outside of this thought-constructed reality. Here's how: Begin by consciously placing your attention on something (anything will serve to begin with) outside this circle of thoughts and feelings.

As a quick example of how this is done, in a moment from now, once you've finished reading the instructions that follow, just break your attention away from this page for a moment. In this same moment, give your newly available awareness to something near you in your living space or just outside your window. Maybe you'll see a bird or tree; or gazing across the room, perhaps you'll notice a bookshelf, TV, or set of drawers. As you do this, come awake to whatever it is you're gazing upon. By this I mean simply become aware of what you see. Bring it fully into your mind. Once you've completed this part of the exercise, return your attention and awareness back to your reading. Go ahead now and begin, remembering to follow the above instructions.

All right, what just happened? Let's look at just a few of the lessons in this brief inner exercise to see what can be learned from them.

First, can you see now that while you had been engaged in reading this text, before you broke away from it, that you had had no real awareness of that tree, table, or desk? So that—in the same instant of your directed "awakening" to its nearby existence—you also became aware of another fact: this choice of yours existed all along in "another reality." By this term I mean simply to say that the reality of that table or tree was quite apart from the one you'd been absorbed in prior to looking up from this page.

Just a bit more consideration of your experience and the lesson will appear. Can you also see that you already have some form of relationship with this same subject?

Of course you do! Maybe you rake up the leaves from that tree each fall; or it could be that your table belonged to your great aunt, and has been handed down from one generation to the next. Whatever the case, here's the point: What you selected to see not only has its "life" outside the field of your formerly focused thoughts, but it belongs to a reality beyond these same thoughts. And further, that this newly perceived reality has its own "history;" an invisible reality that's connected to a greater reality still.

What power can this new and more encompassing awareness grant to you? How can momentarily connecting your attention to some other reality help you to step outside the circle of stress?

Invite the Light That Liberates

Please think through the next set of insights until the view they reveal becomes a part of your own inner vision. Then the truth they illuminate will, indeed, go before you and show you the way out of your stress. The only way any troubling thoughts can continue to provide you with their victim-pro-ducing view of events is to hold your attention riv-eted upon their conditioned standpoint while whispering to you what this means to your life. In this way, their reality is not only passed off on you as being yours, but no other reality exists for you because of this closed circle.

The key here is that this stress-filled circle has no authority to keep you within its influences apart from what you don't understand about its reality. This means that knowing the truth of it is the same as freedom from it. Consciously placing your attention on something outside of this circle is the same as connecting yourself to a reality that's not a part of your presently stressed one. And in this moment of heightened awareness you can see by the light of your increased understand-ing that there is a greater, wider reality to your life than what you had taken to be the whole of your-self only seconds before. This brings us to the last step in our study of how to find complete freedom from stress.

Imagine a man who has been locked in a dark-ened room all of his life; a room with uneven objects in it that never stop moving around, so that this man never knows what these things are— where they move to—and when he will trip and fall down again.

Then, one day, a small, thin shaft of light breaks into the world of his dark room.

At first, the man mistakes this strange brightness to be one of his hidden and ever-shifting tormentors. But soon he begins to see the difference in this new creature by fact of its very nature. His visitor is not a part of the room's conspiracy to hurt him. It's not a part of the hidden things, or of what hides them. No, instead it reveals them. So even though he has no idea what this light is, he does know one thing for sure; it's his friend. He's glad for it. He sees there's safety within it and he's attracted to it.

But his contentment soon gives way to a host of persistent questions, all of which share the same theme and that disturb his newly found peace of mind. From where did this light come? Is there more to it than this beam? And if this small shaft alone can dispel the cause of some of his fears, what would more of it be able to do? Is there somewhere he can live with no darkness in it? Finally, these questions tilt the balance of his formerly fearful reasoning, and he decides to walk toward the source of this light.

Being empowered to step outside the circle of stress becomes possible only as you awaken to see that you're a captive within it; that whatever escape plans your stressed self suggests are not, in fact, solutions to your stress, but are actually symptoms of this stressful circle. This new inner knowledge is the first shaft of light in the darkened room of self. It doesn't speak to us of mere temporary relief from our stresses, but of complete release from the self that causes them. With this inner Light, escape becomes possible. Without it, all the greater becomes the darkness as its shadows of blame, guilt, fear and anger, gather and grow in the shut-tered room of self-ignorance.

Let's pause here for a moment to review our dis-coveries; to reflect upon what we now know as being true about stress, its cause, and its cure.

We've learned that our experience of any given moment is based upon what we're given to see as the reality of it, and that this reality depends entirely upon what we are aware of in the moment.

We've seen that it's possible to wake up to our-selves and to catch stressful thoughts in the act of creating their pressure-filled circle around us; that we can recognize this conflicted state-of-self for what it is; a temporary condition produced in our mind by the activated principles we learned about at the outset of this study: Attraction, Separation, Isolation, Amplification, Machination.

We've also discovered that each time we can remember ourselves in the face of these deceptive inner forces, and see their formations for what they are, that it becomes possible for us to step outside of this stressful circle.

Lastly, from our new studies we know that whatever captures our awareness also fashions, more or less, what we perceive as our reality. But we also know now that anytime we're awake inwardly enough we can choose to consciously direct this same awareness. We can hold it where and upon what we wish, which, in turn, can help us to change what we take as being real. So when we perceive ourselves as being a captive in some circle of stressful thoughts, we can deliberately bring into our consciousness—in that same moment—the awareness of something outside this circle. And if we'll hold our awareness there, take a deep breath and just let go of whatever thoughts may have been defining our sense of self the moment before, we instantly exit our formerly stressed-out self and the thought-produced reality responsible for it. In what can be only an instant of inner work we then find ourselves standing in a new world untouched by stress. But, to complete this journey to a life that's truly stress-free, we need to cover one last important idea.

Take the Steps To the Stress-less Life

It should be clear by now that our experience of life is intimately connected to the way in which we view it, and further that this view changes from moment to moment depending upon what we are relating to within ourselves in each moment.

When we see only our own ideas about why we're feeling stressed, and they're telling us how we're entitled to be miserable, misery makes up the circle of our lives. But when we actually see, within ourselves, that misery loves company, and that we've become its closest friend, we're well on our way to making a new and true friend; to establishing a new relationship with life based in a reality that will not only give us a whole new experience of life, but if this friendship is made fast, we'll come upon a whole new self within ourselves that never feels despair or defeat.

Who is this powerful new friend? The Light of our new understanding whose glimpse into the actual nature of any stressful state is the same as its dismissal. How can this little bit of Light dismiss what may be a lifetime of living in the dark?

Think about the man in our story whose life, until a small streak of light penetrated it, was limited to the reality of his one darkened room.

At first, his relationship with this breaking light was to be suspicious of it, but he soon turned from being fearful to feeling grateful for its liberating presence in his little world. It didn't take him too long to realize that the life he longed for was to live within this Light that had changed his once fearful reality.

As the Light of your new self-understanding expands because of your work with this special exercise, you will discover how stress is created and how, up until now, has been able to keep you its captive. And as this new awareness dawns within you, with each successive gleaning, you will repeatedly, increasingly, see for yourself, within yourself, the evidence of another reality, of another world within you that's outside the circle of stress you've come to think of as being yourself.

Learn to look at all difficult moments as opportunities to come awake to yourself and a place from which you can practice stepping outside of the attending circle of stressful thoughts. In this way, work for yourself and upon yourself. Do your part and be assured that great day of days will come when your developing awareness will forever shift from the unwanted world of your stressful life to the world of inner Light. Within its incorruptible reality awaits that safe haven on earth wherein full and final freedom from stress is already yours.

Helpful Reminders for Higher Self-Study

1. Freedom from the prison of thought begins with being free to think, and you cannot freely consider your own condition if you have a vested interest in remaining you.

2. Stress is an unseen killer that crushes its victims with the pressure of their own thoughts.

3. Real detachment is not won by struggling against attachments, nor is it disdain for possessions, but occurs naturally for the one who has seen that no opposite can cancel its own manifestation.

4. To be in the moment revealed, without understanding that your nature is part of its revelation, is to not only miss realizing your own essential existence but those imperative life-lessons which alone change field, seed, sower, and harvest.

5. The next time you find yourself in a rush to get something finished, try to recollect that freedom doesn't have speeds.

> *As long as anything in this world*
> *means anything to you,*
> *your freedom is only a word.*
> *You are like a bird that is held*
> *by a leash;*
> *you can only fly so far.*
>   —Francis Fenelon

Ten Lights Along the Way

You are not alone in your quest for a life free of stress, strain, and worry. Others have gone before you. Their words, though aged in years, ring new with the timeless truths you're invited to make as your own. Allow the following short list of Ten Lights Along the Way to serve you in your search for freedom. Each of them provides guidance, encouragement, and a special kind of spiritual nourishment needed for the new life.

1. *We do not keep the outward form of order, where there is deep disorder in the mind.*

   —William Shakespeare

2. *For God hath not given us the spirit of fear.*

   —New Testament

3. *The being who has attained harmony, and every being may attain it, has found his place in the order of the universe and represents the divine thought as clearly as a flower or a solar system. Harmony seeks nothing outside itself. It is what it ought to be; it is the expression*

of right, order, law and truth; it is greater than time, and represents eternity.

—Henri Amiel

4. *Do not be bewildered by the surfaces: in the depths all becomes law.*

—Rainer Maria Rilke

5. *If he falls in this conflict, then he falls by his own hand; for physically and externally understood, I can fall by the hand of another, but spiritually there is only one who can destroy me, and that is myself.*

—Soren Kierkegaard

6. *Mark how to know yourself. To know himself a man must ever be on the watch over himself, holding his outer faculties. The object is to reach a state of consciousness—a new state of one self. It is to reach now, where one is present to oneself. What I say unto you I say unto all, be awake.*

—Meister Eckhart

7. *He who has gotten rid of the disease of 'tomorrow' has a chance of achieving what he is here for.*

—George Gurdjieff

8. *O thou that pinest in the imprisonment of the Actual, and criest bitterly to the gods for a kingdom wherein to rule and create, know this for a truth: the thing thou seekest is already here, 'here or nowhere,' couldst thou only see.*

—Thomas Carlyle

9. *Self-government is indeed, the noblest rule on earth; the object of a loftier ambition than the possession of crowns or scepters.*

—John Caird

10. *Bring all of yourself to his door: bring only a part, and you've brought nothing at all.*

—Hakim Sanai

Chapter Seventeen

Principles and Practices for Winning the Higher Life

THERE IS ONE PASSAGE FOUND IN ALL the great scriptures of the world that tells the same truth regardless of time, country, or language. The exact words that dress this eternal principle vary, but the message it conveys is unmistakable. To paraphrase this timeless tenet: *Few find the way; fewer walk it; fewer still are they who enter into real life.*

Before we go any farther, don't discount this truth, thinking it applies only to those who aspire to some impossible spiritual life. This conclusion would be a tragic error. As you'll see, this great principle has immediate consequences for anyone wishing to live in a higher, brighter world. Let's see if this is true.

Over and over again the lessons in the chapters leading up to this one have all pointed us in one basic direction; urging us to consider just how great a secret role real self-knowledge plays in determining our destiny. With this same fundamental insight safely in hand, let's restate the eternal principle mentioned just above by putting it into the context of our study in self-determination.

Few are those content with the direction their lives have taken; fewer are the men and women willing to learn why their destiny feels outside their control; and fewer still are those individuals who persist upon the path of self-discovery until realizing the truth of why their worlds unfold as they do.

One of the sad reasons why so few men and women persist in the inner work necessary for higher self-discovery is because we have all become —to one degree or another—either an unwitting captive of, or willing participant in, what can only be described as a descending scale in the meaning of life.

More simply stated, over time our values have been subtly shifting away from the love of the *wisdom of life* to the excitement of striving to win at life; from the possibility of a self-renewing relationship with eternal forces to the promise of increasingly one-sided interactions with what amounts to little more than the pursuit of temporary possessions.

Only the ignorance of ourselves to what is possible for each of us to actually be, as opposed to what we hope to have—but never seem to secure—could allow such a meaningless state of self to persist and become self-perpetuating. Only self-ignorance would accept a mediocre life as the inescapable conclusion to the deep discontentment inherent in any direction supplied by self-ignorance.

What this proves, if we'll agree to reflect upon the truth being presented, is that higher self-knowledge, real wisdom, represents the rudder we must have to correct the course of this drifting ship we call self. Why? Because the happy truth is that we are not so much lost in the sea of choices life offers us as we are just adrift amongst them; caught up in their ever-changing currents and unsure as to which shore is our homeland. So wisdom is not only the higher course, but our safe harbor as well. Which brings us to a very important idea:

It isn't enough to just learn the principles of wisdom. Studying wise principles without putting them into practice is like learning how to read music but never owning an instrument through which to experience the sound of those notes you know. True wisdom is not theory. It is the fruit of experience whose seed is action. The wise are not those most learned, but the best tempered by truths put to the test of life.

It is essential for any person intending to be more than a leaf in the wind of life to learn the truth of him or herself by boldly jumping into these very same winds. Life, *as it is*—and not as we'd wish it to be—is our school, teacher, and teaching. Each event and relationship therein is our own field, grain, thresher, oven, and bread, making our willingness to dive into life's lessons the determining factor in whether we learn to rise above this world or remain ruled by it. The choice is ours, so the more knowledgeable we are about ourselves the fewer questions we will have about which path we choose.

The following series of questions and answers reveals a number of important principles, practices, and pathways necessary for study by anyone interested in becoming a self-determining individual. For ease of reference, I've divided these new lessons into three special categories according to their subject matter.

Use this last section of our work together to help you see, and then accomplish, three vital inner tasks. *First:* To prove to yourself that just as the absence of self-understanding is the same as standing in darkness, new and true self-knowledge serves as the Light that lights the way. *Second:* If the way, whatever point you may be upon it, can be lit up once, it can be permanently illuminated. *Third:* The ability to see, clearly, the way ahead of you is the same as being empowered to make those choices called determining your own destiny.

One last thought: Refuse to be content with merely being discontented with the direction your life has taken you so far. You can learn to *be* better. All discontentment is a form of unconscious self-compromise, and no one compromises with his or her happiness unless it appears no other choice exists. Now you know there's always a higher choice. Never forget this one great lesson. Choosing to refuse any thought or feeling that's trying to drag you anywhere not only releases you from its downward direction, but frees you to discover, each time you make this choice, that a higher destiny has always been awaiting you. Go to work!

How To Use Difficult People For Your Self-Liberation

Question: In my job I have to deal with many hateful coworkers and other people each day. I can tolerate just so many of these kinds of people per day as we all have to do, but a couple of dozen of them is too many for me to take. What can I do to tolerate this situation besides getting another job?

Response: As difficult as this may be to understand just now, your present work circumstance of being surrounded by "toxic" people is perfect for your continuing development in self-command—if you'll learn how to use it. I say you must learn "how to use it" because if you don't learn this secret then, wherever you go, you'll continue to encounter these types of "hateful" people, and your own negative reactions will not only turn you "toxic," but use up your whole life in the painful process. Try this: Determine when you walk in your office that your attention will remain with your reactions to these people and not upon the people themselves. This shift in your attention will help you realize what it is you really need to be free of, namely yourself! And "need" is the key word in this instance because you'll see, if you'll practice this approach, that even though people can be monstrous at times, it's your response to their behavior that's jumping in to wreck the moment. Once this much is clear, then you can begin the fun inner work of jumping out of your own judgmental self with all of its painful reactions. A happy landing is assured!

Question: Any tips on how to best deal with the-sky-is-falling type personalities? Some people just aren't happy unless there's a crisis to consume their lives and can find some way to drag others into their nightmare.

Response: The way to deal with any anxious individuals in our lives begins with learning to walk away from those crisis-causing thoughts and feelings in our own nature. None of us can be any more effective in our outer life than we are awake within ourselves. The inner determines the outer. One good beginning for ending wrong relationships with anxious thoughts or people is to be willing to be without the false identity that either causes. Work at this.

Question: After certain negative events, the feeling of wanting to exact revenge on the perpetrator—in order to regain peace of mind—can be very strong. This wish to "fix" those at fault remains with me for a long time. Will these thoughts dissipate with the right inner work?

Response: Yes, they will. And here's some extra help to speed up the healing you wish for. Thoughts of revenge promise to relieve the mind they occupy of the painful pressure these same thoughts produce. However, this self-supplied perception is a total deception. *All* acts of revenge are not only useless, but destroy the one who acts from them. These are not just words. If you'll refuse to give dark thoughts and feelings your life for a long enough period, they will reveal themselves to you as being the secret destroyers that they are. I promise you that such negativity has no life outside of the one that they're able to trick you into giving them. Rob yourself of their promised relief enough times and the day will come when you'll know the real relief of being free from the whole false idea of revenge.

Question: I know some people who, every day it seems, make cutting remarks just for their own weird personal enjoyment. How can I get them to stop?

Response: One of the reasons (albeit it unknown to the very ones who do this attacking) that some people pounce upon others the way they do, is that they are feeding off of us in many different ways.

This psycho/spiritual phenomena is especially true when we are asleep to ourselves and return one negative energy for another. If you'd like an amazing experience, try sometime consciously refusing your own negativity in the face of someone else's. How? Just go inwardly and outwardly quiet, sit back within yourself, and watch what happens to the person who has "attacked" you. You'll be shocked to see this person lose his "balance" right in the middle of his attack. And even if he or she doesn't actually change the way they behave, your increased self-wisdom about these kind of wars will leave you feeling in much greater control of yourself and your destiny.

Question: At my workplace there is an employee who will never agree with anything anybody has to say. He has a negative attitude toward people and events that make it almost impossible to work with him. How can I prevent his attitude from entering into me?

Response: The only real way to win this struggle is to refuse to fight with his negative influences regardless of what form they may take. Be awake, instead, to the fact that within you there must still be corresponding parts upon which his negativity finds soil and nourishment. Remember two things here: The hatred of hatred is not love; and always strive first to examine the inner self before setting out to change the outer situation.

Turn Any Negative Force Into A Power For Your Freedom

Question: Even though I can reason that stressful thoughts must be a lie, I often see their insistence as evidence of their truthfulness. So much so, that many times it's difficult to distinguish which of my thoughts are true and which are false. Can you give me some insights that will help make distinguishing between the two easier?

Response: Here's one good way to judge the difference between what are true and false thoughts (and this goes for emotions, too). First, and always, come awake to yourself and observe, as best you can, whether the thoughts at hand are there to serve you or to steal from you. Here's what I mean by this idea: Thoughts that serve us are of two basic, but distinct, natures. First, there's practical thoughts for our everyday living. Then we can have higher thoughts; those that help us to better understand ourselves or to see more deeply into this life. On the other hand, thoughts that steal from us are those that promise one thing and deliver another. For example, anxious thoughts always steal. They promise if we will obey their instructions, that we'll escape the punishment in the anxiety. These thoughts do not end anxiety, but keep alive the unconscious nature from which they arise.

Question: Whenever some bad news arrives via telephone or mail, I immediately forget all that I've learned and turn into a fearful mess. In an instant the pounding of my heart drums out all good sense and I'm right back to my old ways and old self. What can I do?

Response: Strangely enough, waking up to discover that we've forgotten what we thought we knew is the beginning of a new and higher kind of knowing. Let me explain. For many years, rightfully so, we'll struggle to meet our "shaky" moments with solid spiritual principles. But these higher ideas about fearless living are still just at the level of thought. In other words, right ideas are still of a thought nature which places them at the same level as the thoughts attacking us. We must learn this inner reality the hard way, which as we do, gradually teaches us to stop resisting these negative states all together. Remember: Our new aim is not to somehow "overpower" stressful states, but to dwell inwardly where these troubled thoughts are powerless to punish us.

Question: I'm beginning to see how thought creates the opposites, especially when it comes to trying to control my desires. But how on earth do you get above these things? The more I try and control my thoughts, the stronger the resistance. If you do nothing, then nothing changes. Help!

Response: What you must eventually see if you want to be free is this: The part of you that wants to control desire is itself but an opposite of that desire you're trying to control. The only way to truly end the tyranny of any desire is to realize that the only thing really being satisfied by its longing is its longing to find satisfaction in this longing. In other words, desires have no end to themselves if we pursue their ends. As these facts become clear, letting go of longings becomes easier.

Question: Anxiety seems to be my lot in life lately. I have a full plate of activities with children, a challenging job, and a few outside interests. However, as much as I feel like I balance these and keep my priorities straight, I'm still visited often by anxiety that seems to have been triggered by worries over these same issues. Any suggestions on how I can get clear of this contradiction?

Response: Anxiety can be one of the more difficult internal states to work with because of its highly deceptive operating system. The key to escaping its captivity begins with realizing this one truth about it: The only real influence any anxious state has over you is its promise of relief from *what* you're stressed about *if* you'll do what the state is compelling you to do about *it*. Of course, once you yield to this pressure, and take steps toward the offending event seen as its cause, the pressure within you does seem to lessen. But, as time soon reveals, the one constant through all changing conditions is that your own anxious nature remains. It is this very insight that empowers you to take the power out of all anxious states. Here's how to start. When you understand that *anxious states live for themselves*, at your expense, then you can begin acting toward their appearance within you with what *you* know is true about their nature instead of listening to what this pressure is telling you is true about you. The clearer this becomes to you, the sooner you'll stop giving yourself away to anxious states.

Question: Why do I seem to like my confusion so much? If it's true that each of us has in our life what we really want, I must really want this confusion, because I always find myself loaded with it!

Response: Seeing that something in you likes confusion is the first step in bringing an end to it, but you need new knowledge that you must work with to bring it to an end. Consider this: Confusion is really a runaway play of opposites, where one thought arrives at a seeming conclusion only to be replaced by another thought that calls it into doubt and then suggests another way to look at the same problem. The real problem is this thought-nature whose drive mechanism is the back-and-forth operation of the opposites—and whose secret intention is to keep alive the false sense of self that this internal and infernal dialog keeps going. See all of this and then dare to step out of this strained circle of self. Knowing, with greater and greater clarity that you can't find freedom within it, will help you to drop it.

Question: Could you give some insight into loneliness and how to abolish it?

Response: Loneliness is not the problem. Fear of loneliness is what drives us into wrong relationships, and despairing of ourselves. Think about it. The feeling of being alone has no negative content in and of itself. But as the mind works on it, and brings to bear all of the past negative experiences about being lonely, suddenly loneliness turns from a lamb into a lion. We can never be free of any negative state without being willing to meet it, to see it fully. Negative states continue to win the day and our lives because we don't face them truthfully.

One great spiritual secret is that if we come aware of ourselves and consciously dare dark states to do their worst to us, the Light will come to our defense. And in these enlightened moments, we are released; not from being by ourselves but from the aching illusion that being alone somehow precludes the possibility of feeling happy and complete within ourselves.

Question: Can you help me handle depression? I'm so weary of being so weary, but I'm at a loss over my own condition. Is there a way out?

Response: Oh yes. Try this simple inner exercise to exorcise any dark state. The next time depression comes to take you over, think *toward it*, instead of *from it*. What this means is that you're to realize in the moment of being taken over by the darkness that you are simply wrongly involved in thinking about your state from the state itself. This is exactly how negative states take us captive. See any depressed state as an imposition being thrust upon you, instead of just unconsciously accepting its "unlife" as your own. Work at this. Your efforts will be rewarded.

Question: I not only stiffen up sometimes before speaking to someone who intimidates me, but sometimes I feel like my throat is choking up with so much tension I'm afraid I'll lose the power to even speak! I'd very much like to get past this debilitating, sometimes humiliating, state of self. What can I do?

Response: If we're ever to outgrow the predicaments that we face, we must not allow these trials to dictate to us our choices. In this instance, whenever we run into areas that are challenging, a part of us urges us to avoid these situations. This is exactly the wrong choice. The right one is to go into the challenge ahead and not let the problem steer us away from seeing into its real cause. The wrong parts of ourselves are always defining us according to the limitations that they secretly are. In this instance, anything that we fear, or that makes us behave oddly, will tell us that it's the person or the situation that is causing us this conflict. We must always remember that in all circumstances, our situation is ourselves. And that it is through direct contact with these parts and doing what they fear to do that will prove to us there was nothing real in the fear. All fear, all negative states, are conditional. This means that if we stay the course, remaining aware of ourselves even as these parts threaten us, we will see these fears fade and disappear.

Inspiring Points and Helpful Powers Along the Path to Self-Success

Question: Why is it that whenever we remember to come awake and actually "see" fearful thoughts and feelings for what they are, they seem to be so much less intimidating?

Response: Your question points the way to a vital inner principle. We've learned that the quality of our inner life is determined by what we are in relationship with our inner selves in any given moment. The very attempt *to see* a fear, as opposed to just unconsciously accepting it, changes our whole inner relationship with this condition. Even just one right idea about the true nature of fear placed in your mind at the same moment a fear enters into it diminishes that fear. Naturally, the next moment is higher.

Question: What is the best way to "make up" for wrongs you have done in the past to others (betraying, lying, stealing, etc.)?

Response: Truth be known, until we wake up, we are all in one form or another of wrong relationship with even those we love which means . . . none of us are exempt from wronging others.

That's why the key to correcting what we consider to be a faulty past is to work to be awake in the present. The wrong parts of us want to keep themselves alive by continually dragging before our mind's eye all that we have been wrong in doing. Then we react to these images, and in one form or another start resisting them, which secretly continues both their lives and our wrong behavior. Drop all of your concerns for what is no longer, and be intent on being conscious of what is before you in each present moment. This new kind of mindfulness changes not only the way in which we relate to our "past" regrets, but it alters the course of our future. Here's a nice idea; we don't have to regret a mistake we don't make!

Question: Sometimes I feel overwhelmed by all the things one must do to get a better handle on life. Isn't there a simpler approach to self-command?

Response: One of the earliest and most important lessons that all of us must embrace, over and over again, is to learn what it means to work with what is in our power, and to not be taken over by trying to deal with what is not in our power. For instance, it isn't in our power to make flooding emotions settle down by any form of resisting them or wishing them to go away. What is in our power is to recognize that despairing emotions have their own agenda, namely, to keep their feeling of discouragement alive and to keep us in conflict over our seeming inability to resolve this ache. Drop any feelings of yourself that seems to tell you discouraging things about yourself. These sinking states are not yours and neither is the self that feels compelled to struggle with them.

Question: I have followed esoteric studies for several years now and I've had what I'd call "moments" of spiritual awakening. Yet, these moments seem to fade back into a murmur all too quickly. When these moments arise, I have a new depth of clarity, silence, and self-command. Are there any specific lessons to apply during these moments to help anchor myself there? It would seem that at that special time, more powerful anchors could be realized.

Response: Nothing is more priceless than those moments when we suddenly are able to see that the world that we took as being everything was only a small part of a greater something. Suddenly, we realize we indeed dwell within ourselves within a much larger world than we could have hoped existed. When these "awakenings" come, it seems natural to want to hang onto them, but consider the following: Isn't it true that each of these illuminating moments came to you unannounced? And that it was the presence of this new Light within you that awakened you to itself and to all that it revealed? Now, "you" want to be the one who possesses this Light and who can call upon it at will. This "you" is what stands between "you" and the Light you long for. As difficult as it is to do, you must work to let go of your wish to return to any moment once glimpsed in favor of being open to the onset of a whole new Light.

Question: What can I do to help myself discover more about myself that will change my life? I want to be awake, but have trouble identifying ways to keep the wish alive.

Response: Try and make a point to bring yourself back to an awake state as many times a day as you can. There are helpful ways to do this. Set simple tasks for yourself that when you do them, part of doing them requires you remembering yourself. For instance, at the office, make it your aim to know you're reaching for the phone when you reach for it. When someone hands you something, know that you've taken it from his or her hand. Turn off the radio or TV right in the middle of your favorite part! You'll come awake! The more of these special kind of internal alarm clocks you can set for yourself, the more awakenings are possible.

Question: I have the problem of looking for myself in other people's eyes (which I know I shouldn't do). What purpose should other people fill in our lives?

Response: When we view this life as the school for higher education it's intended to be, then every relationship is a classroom. But with our present view, life has become a kind of popularity contest; so that within this context everyone we meet is seen as either a potential ally in our cause, or as an enemy to be avoided. Either way, we are made a victim of this misperception. When our purpose is to wake up, then every relationship, regardless of how someone else sees us, serves to help us see the next step in our own development.

Question: I love the whole idea of being awake . . . especially when it comes to what course is best to take in life in any given moment. But why is it so hard to come awake to myself and stay there?

Response: In order for any person to "wake up" (let's just use that expression), he or she must come to grips with what the teachings down through the ages have called the "sleeping self." This lower nature is asleep in itself, and to itself, moving through life in a dream that it calls life. It exists perpetually in this dream state, content to

161

resist its alternating nightmares and cling to its excitements. For those of us who wish to awaken, the key is to understand that we are, at present, fully in the hands of this sleeping self that doesn't want anything to disturb its slumber. As we wake up to our actual inner condition, and begin seeing the actual self-defeat inherent in our unconscious state, then what's seen as being difficult isn't coming "awake" but how hard it is on us (and everyone else) for us to remain asleep! This dawning self-discovery strengthens both our wish to come awake and the higher will needed to succeed.

Question: After reading your work *The Secret of Letting Go*, I finally tried practicing some of its principles. I was overstressed at work and I decided to just let it go and handle one thing at a time as best I knew how. I was amazed to find energy that I hadn't felt in years. But it didn't last. Do we have to continue letting go of things to keep that feeling of energy?

Response: It's true. Our energy is wrongly spent battling windmills. When we awaken, even a little bit, and begin walking out of the crowd of thoughts—letting them go instead of trying to control them—all of that wonderful energy essential to our true sense of self returns to rule the roost. It radiates the natural health and strong sense of well-being that only it is capable of providing in us. And now, a question for you. Your response will answer what you've asked me. What person, finding a buried chest of gold, takes only a few coins home with him when, with just a bit of extra work, he can possess the whole hidden treasure? Right! I know you'll keep working.

Question: What's your opinion about goal setting? Do you think traditional success advice about visualizing and modeling successful people has any real value?

Response: Everything depends on what we really want from this life. Being a self-commanding person has little to do with redesigning failed past models or envisioning future ambitions, but with being awake to those timeless energies within us whose very existence—and upward direction—we're each invited to join. Besides, as author Vernon Howard once told a small gathering of students, "It is wise to seek immortality because time defeats all other ambitions."

Question: In a nutshell, what *is* our true nature?

Response: It can never really be spoken of; only realized in varying degrees, depending upon the individual's receptivity. But let's consider just a few characteristics of this true nature as an awakened person might experience them. They include an abiding sense of the eternal that is never apart from one's own self. The direct knowledge that "you" are somehow situated in the center of the universe and, as such, that everything in life is not only created just for you, but waits for you to claim it. And certainly not last, and by no means least, a deep awareness of participating in a great purpose and plan to life coupled with an unshakable confidence that nothing can interfere with its success.

Question: Are failures in life inevitable?

Response: Try and understand the difference between living from something within yourself whose nature is contentment itself, and living from those parts of yourself that are forever seeking contentment. For those who persist with their wish of self-discovery—who will put this love of the Light first in their lives—there really is no such thing as failure. Why? Because every event—regardless of its "apparent" outcome, reveals to these sincere seekers what was formerly unknown to them . . . about themselves. That's the key! The only thing that stands between us and the higher self we all strive to be, is what we don't understand about the nature of the "barrier" before us. And all such barriers, all, are constructed out of what we've yet to learn about ourselves. This means that self-discovery is self-success, and that for the self-studying man or women, failure simply ceases to exist!

Question: I find your idea about wishing to learn something new and true about ourselves every day so exciting! What a way to live! To wake up every morning with such a wish has become my greatest hope. What must I do to make this wish my reality?

Response: With persistence on your part, with a conscious refusal to accept no substitute for the contentment, confidence, and strength only higher self-understanding can provide, in no time at all it will be a new world that will come *to wake you up* every morning! You may be assured these words are not just some wishful affirmation. They state the crowning fact of the higher life. Anyone who will ask for real life, and then dare to learn what this authentic life requires of him or her, will also win that destiny long dreamed about; everything that's needed to be happy is *already* right where you are.

Special Summary

The hardest spiritual lesson learned: What's borrowed must be returned!

I laugh when I hear that the fish in the water is thirsty. You don't grasp the fact that what is most alive of all is inside your own house; and so you walk from one holy city to the next with a confused look!

—Kabir

Chapter Eighteen

Set Your Sights on Self-Liberation

THE TWELVE INNER-LIFE STEPS described in this book share one life-changing objective: They are all about awakening you to new and higher levels of yourself through increased self-awareness. But as you proceed with your studies and practices, please keep this one, very important, fact before your inquiring mind. There is no scale, no measuring stick for this new inner awareness. You cannot measure it any more than you can measure the cosmos.

What this means is that in our inner work to awaken and realize ourselves, we must begin where we begin, and put away any other concerns about where that beginning is. It's enough just to make a start, wherever that may be. What difference does it make at what point you enter into a great river? Sooner or later, all its waters reach and pour into the sea.

Never let discouragement have the final word and one day there will be nothing left to discuss. Besides, you can have just as many new beginnings as you're willing to leave behind all your ideas about yourself. Nothing in this world, or in any other, can stop you from discovering your original, free Being. This has always been your destiny, as Walt Whitman confirms:

"The central urge in every atom [is] to return to its divine source and origin."

As a final review and summary of the important lessons in this book, following are ten secret ways higher self-studies can help you succeed in life.

1. Higher self-studies reveal that your nature is your fortune, so better luck begins with a change of self.

2. Higher self-studies hold many benefits for the sincere student, like the deep-sea diver who discovers a treasure chest lying buried beneath a bed of pearls.

3. Higher self-studies introduce your mind to a higher body of wisdom whose elevated nature lifts you, as wind does the wings of an eagle.

4. Higher self-studies prove that permitting your life direction to be determined by the way the world turns is like using the pointer of a wind-lashed weathervane for your compass and guide.

5. Higher self-studies prove that changing the way you see your life changes the life you see.

6. Higher self-studies pave the happy and relief-filled way to a new life that isn't governed by ceaseless compromise and painful self-interest.

7. Higher self-studies reveal secret sources of conflict, as in discovering that the chief thief responsible for stealing your peace of mind is your own certainty that you already know the real nature of security.

8. Higher self-studies provide superior self-safety by helping you develop a new awareness that can see through highly reflective surfaces, such as well-polished personalities that conceal hidden motives.

9. Higher self-studies teach you the wisdom of letting go, which has nothing to do with giving up on your life—or into self-defeating desires.

10. Higher self-studies make it clear that looking for a sense of self-permanence in the way others think about you is like trying to make a plaster cast of the wind.

☽ REACH FOR THE MOON

Llewellyn publishes hundreds of books on your favorite subjects! To get these exciting books, including the ones on the following pages, check your local bookstore or order them directly from Llewellyn.

ORDER BY PHONE
- Call toll-free within the U.S. and Canada, 1-800-THE MOON
- In Minnesota, call (651) 291-1970
- We accept VISA, MasterCard, and American Express

ORDER BY MAIL
- Send the full price of your order (MN residents add 7% sales tax) in U.S. funds, plus postage & handling to:

  Llewellyn Worldwide
  P.O. Box 64383, Dept. K282-8
  St. Paul, MN 55164–0383, U.S.A.

POSTAGE & HANDLING
(For the U.S., Canada, and Mexico)
- $4.00 for orders $15.00 and under
- $5.00 for orders over $15.00
- No charge for orders over $100.00

We ship UPS in the continental United States. We ship standard mail to P.O. boxes. Orders shipped to Alaska, Hawaii, The Virgin Islands, and Puerto Rico are sent first-class mail. Orders shipped to Canada and Mexico are sent surface mail.

International orders: Airmail—add freight equal to price of each book to the total price of order, plus $5.00 for each non-book item (audio tapes, etc.).

Surface mail—Add $1.00 per item.

Allow 2 weeks for delivery on all orders.
Postage and handling rates subject to change.

DISCOUNTS
We offer a 20% discount to group leaders or agents. You must order a minimum of 5 copies of the same book to get our special quantity price.

FREE CATALOG
Get a free copy of our color catalog, *New Worlds of Mind and Spirit*. Subscribe for just $10.00 in the United States and Canada ($30.00 overseas, airmail). Many bookstores carry *New Worlds*—ask for it!

Visit our web site at www.llewellyn.com for more information.

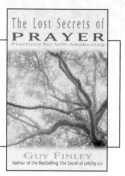

The Lost Secrets of Prayer
Practices for Self-Awakening

Guy Finley

Do your prayers go unanswered? Or when they are answered, do the results bring you only temporary relief or happiness? If so, you may be surprised to learn that there are actually two kinds of prayer, and the kind that most of us practice is actually the least effective.

Best-selling author Guy Finley presents *The Lost Secrets of Prayer*, a guide to the second kind of prayer. The purpose of true prayer, as revealed in the powerful insights that make up this book, is not to appeal for what you think you want. Rather, it is to bring you to the point where you are no longer blocked from seeing that everything you need is already here. When you begin praying in this new way, you will discover a higher awareness of your present self. Use these age-old yet forgotten practices for self-awakening and your life will never be the same.

1-56718-276-3
240 pp., 5¼ x 8 $9.95

The Intimate Enemy
Winning the War Within Yourself

Guy Finley and Ellen Dickstein

Within each of us lurk invisible psychological characters that inhabit our inner beings and make choices for us—choices that repeatedly cause us pain on some level. Now, best-selling self-help author Guy Finley and psychologist Dr. Ellen Dickstein expose these characters for what they really are: our mechanical, unconscious reactions and misperceptions that create a threatening world.

The Intimate Enemy will introduce you to astounding parts of yourself that you never knew existed. You will observe the inner dramas that control your life without your knowledge. Best of all, you will awaken to a higher awareness that provides the only true strength and confidence you need to walk into a fearless future. As you uncover the exciting truth about who you really are, you will gain an unshakable understanding of the human struggle and witness proof of a higher world, free from all strife.

1-56718-279-8
256 pp., 5³⁄₁₆ x 8 $9.95

To order, call 1-800-THE MOON
Prices subject to change without notice

The Secret of Letting Go

Guy Finley

Whether you need to let go of a painful heartache, a destructive habit, a frightening worry or a nagging discontent, *The Secret of Letting Go* shows you how to call upon your own hidden powers and how they can take you through and beyond any challenge or problem. This book reveals the secret source of a brand-new kind of inner strength.

In the light of your new and higher self-understanding, emotional difficulties such as loneliness, fear, anxiety and frustration fade into nothingness as you happily discover they never really existed in the first place.

With a foreword by Desi Arnaz Jr., and introduction by Dr. Jesse Freeland, *The Secret of Letting Go* is a pleasing balance of questions and answers, illustrative examples, truth tales, and stimulating dialogues that allow the reader to share in the exciting discoveries that lead up to lasting self-liberation.

0-87542-223-3
240 pp., 5¼ x 8 $9.95

To order, call 1-800-THE MOON
Prices subject to change without notice

**Freedom from the
Ties that Bind**
The Secret of Self Liberation

Guy Finley

Discover an inner world of wisdom and make miracles happen! Here is a simple yet deeply effective system of illuminating and eliminating the problems of inner mental and emotional life.

In *Freedom from the Ties that Bind*, Guy Finley reveals hundreds of Celestial, but down-to-earth, secrets of Self-Liberation that show you exactly how to be fully independent, and free of any condition not to your liking. Even the most difficult people won't be able to turn your head or test your temper. Enjoy solid, meaningful relationships founded in conscious choice—not through self-defeating compromise. Learn the secrets of unlocking the door to your own Free Mind. Be empowered to break free of any self-punishing pattern, and make the discovery that who you really are is already everything you've ever wanted to be.

0-87542-217-9
240 pp., 6 x 9 $10.00

To order, call 1-800-THE MOON
Prices subject to change without notice

The Secret Way of Wonder

Insights from the Silence

Guy Finley

Discover an inner world of wisdom and make miracles happen! Here is a simple yet deeply effective system of illuminating and eliminating the problems of inner mental and emotional life.

The Secret Way of Wonder is an interactive spiritual workbook, offering guided practice for self-study. It is about Awakening the Power of Wonder in yourself. A series of 60 "Wonders" (meditations on a variety of subjects: "The Wonder of Change," "The Wonder of Attachments," etc.) will stir you in an indescribable manner. This is a bold and bright new kind of book that gently leads us on a journey of Spiritual Alchemy where the journey itself is the destination . . . and the destination is our need to be spiritually whole men and women. With an Introduction by Desi Arnaz, Jr.

0-87542-221-7

192 pp., 5¼ x 8 $9.95